Research with Children
Perspectives and Practices

Edited by Pia Christensen and Allison James

London and New York

First published 2000 by Falmer Press
11 New Fetter Lane, London EC4P 4EE

Simultaneously published in the USA and Canada
by Falmer Press
Garland Inc, 19 Union Square West, New York, NY 10003

Reprinted 2001, 2002, 2003 by RoutledgeFalmer

RoutledgeFalmer is an imprint of the Taylor & Francis Group

Typeset in Times by BC Typesetting, Bristol
Printed and bound in Great Britain by
Biddles Ltd, Guildford and King's Lynn

British Library Cataloguing in Publication Data
A catalogue record for this book is available from the British Library

Library of Congress Cataloguing in Publication Data
A catalog record for this book has been requested

ISBN 0–750–70975–8 (hbk)
ISBN 0–750–70974–X (pbk)

Introduction

Researching Children and Childhood: Cultures of Communication

Pia Christensen and Allison James

Background

One can find out about something in a number of different ways. However, in any kind of social research, knowing what questions to ask and the ways in which it is best to ask them, as well as knowing which questions *not* to ask and how *not* to ask them, is recognized as one of the keys to a successful research outcome. Indeed, acknowledgement of these and other issues of communication is now the cornerstone of reflexive research practice within many, if not all, social science disciplines. It is a central issue, for example, in the continuing debate within social anthropology about forms of self-presentation and other-representation throughout the research process (Marcus and Fischer 1986; Hastrup 1995). In other disciplines similar questions are being raised, fronted in particular by concerns generated through feminist approaches to research (Caplan 1988). Within the social study of childhood a comparable questioning has taken place (Alanen 1988), generated by the concern that children's voices have traditionally been 'muted' within the social sciences (Hardman 1973). However, as Christensen (1994: 4) argues, 'changing the position of children in the social and cultural sciences requires a re-examination of the conceptual frameworks that influence children's representation'. This book enters into these debates through exploring the methodologies of representation adopted by those conducting research within what has come to be called the new social studies of childhood.

Our engagement with these issues is not straightforward for, despite its coverage of a variety of methods and a range of disciplinary perspectives, this book does not present a Cook's tour of *how* best to carry out research with children. Indeed, in some ways, its intention is completely other – no rules of sociological method are to be found here. And here are no well-tested recipes with formulas guaranteeing a successful result. Rather, the book sets out to explore the complexity of the epistemological and methodological questions that arise in contemporary research practices with children.

1

Exploring such issues is, we suggest, critical in a field of study where researchers are increasingly having to address the theoretical and policy implications of treating children as social actors in their own right in contexts where, traditionally, they have been denied those rights of participation and their voices have remained unheard (James and Prout 1990; Alderson 1995). This does not mean, however, that there will be no practical guidance about conducting research with children to be found – throughout the chapters many insightful lessons can be gained.

This book is, therefore, a book not about methods but about methodologies. It represents a rich collection of contributions from authors with a wide range of disciplinary backgrounds, research practices and theoretical perspectives. We have deliberately chosen this broad diversity in order to represent the, by now, wide field of study which comprises research with children and to illustrate the knowledges that are being produced not only about children's lives through research but also, and importantly, about the process of researching those lives.

The book begins from the assumption that to carry out research with children does not *necessarily* entail adopting different or particular methods – as the individual chapters reveal, like adults, children can and do participate in structured and unstructured interviews; they fill in question-naires; and, on their own terms, they allow the participant observer to join with them in their daily lives. Thus, although some research techniques might sometimes be thought to be more appropriate for use with children, with regard to particular research contexts or the framing of particular research questions, there is, we would argue, nothing particular or indeed peculiar to children that makes the use of any technique imperative. In this sense, this book helps deconstruct the essentialism with which the study of children and childhood has hitherto been regarded and which is already manifested in a shift in the dominant methodological approaches used in childhood research (Woodhead and Faulkner, Chapter 2; Christensen and James, Chapter 8 in this volume).

Traditionally, childhood and children's lives have solely been explored through the views and understandings of their adult caretakers. Such an approach has, in part, been challenged by a perspective which, avowedly child focused, sees children as possessing distinctive cognitive and social developmental characteristics with which researchers, wishing to use child informants, must consider in their research design. A third, and relatively recent approach, forming a new tradition within which this book can be located, suggests, however, that research with children should not take for granted an adult/child distinction. As in all research, what is important is that the particular methods chosen for a piece of research should be appropriate for the people involved in the study, its social and cultural context and the kinds of research questions that have been posed. As Solberg (1996) has argued in justifying her decision to ignore 'age' as a significant marker in her research into child work,

> our concept of such qualities should not influence ways of approaching children in social science research. It should be open to empirical investigation to explore the significance of age and status within different contexts and situations, to explore 'doing' rather than 'being'.
>
> (Solberg 1996: 63–4)

In this book the authors of each chapter set out, therefore, to reflect on and identify how it is that they carry out research with children from a variety of different disciplinary and epistemological positions – from psychology, history, phenomenology, sociology, anthropology and from the standpoint of applied research involved in a variety of policy fields. These different approaches to the study of childhood alert us to the wide variety of theoretical, practical, moral and ethical issues which arise when working with children and exploring childhood through the insights they provide into the framing of research questions, the interpretation of data and the experience of the research process. Notwithstanding these differences in standpoint and intention there are, however, a number of common themes which emerge through the book, themes which, when brought together, go some way to identifying the central methodological planks upon which future research with children can build.

Recounting Paradigm Shifts in Childhood Research

Most contributors to this volume demonstrate in their accounts of researching childhood how a distinct paradigm shift has had implications for the ways in which they undertake their research work within their own particular field of study or in their professional expertise and practice. This shift has involved repositioning children as the subjects, rather than objects of research. While for some this move to recognising children as social actors is implicit and taken-for-granted, other authors have made this shift a distinctive focus for their chapter through revealing the complexities and obstacles that have occurred in this process within their particular discipline. Their accounts testify to the close scrutiny and revamping of earlier research methods and practices which has had to occur in order to facilitate this paradigmatic shift. They also show how sometimes this has entailed making a more personal commitment. Jenks (Chapter 3), on the one hand, through an autobiographical account, details how his own intellectual rootedness in phenomenology enabled him to grasp, early on, the importance within sociology of seeing childhood not as simply the context for socialization but as the frame within which children become constituted as children and also actively constitute themselves. Woodhead and Faulkner's Chapter 1, on the other hand, provides a broad overview of the shifts which have and still are taking place within developmental psychology, noting the obstacles and epistemological barriers which such changes confront. In Hendrick's Chapter 2, it is clear that within history, however, any paradigm shift has yet to really take place. He argues that lessons from the new social studies of childhood – for example that children are social actors in their own right and thus participants in the shaping of social, political, cultural and economic structures – can and must be drawn on by historians, if a new era within childhood history is to be created.

Within the field of policy and practice Roberts' account (Chapter 11) reveals how shifting the perspective on children has manifested itself in children's organizations beginning to involve children themselves in the research process in innovative ways. In drawing a subtle distinction between 'listening' to children and 'hearing' what they say, Roberts argues that although earlier so-called child-focused approaches may have listened to children, researchers and practitioners may often not have heard them. In this way Roberts also draws attention to the important link between theory and practice in order to ensure that the process and outcomes of research are of real benefit and value to children.

The study of childhood as a segment in the life course and as a structural feature of society has been as equally important as research into children's everyday lives in the 'new paradigm' in childhood studies (James and Prout 1990). In Chapter 4, Qvortrup argues that, despite the seeming shift in emphasis towards ethnography as the main tool for exploring children's lives, it is essential also to maintain and further develop macro-comparative perspectives on childhood. These, he argues, enable the more qualitative and micro-analysis of children's everyday lives to be situated, both locally and globally. Through citing in-depth examples of large-scale statistical studies Qvortrup is able to extrapolate factors which contribute to the diversities of childhood and therefore of children's daily lives. In doing so he points to the importance of adopting a generational perspective when considering societal inequalities and socio-political and economic change. This view is confirmed by Scott in Chapter 5. She emphasizes the importance of adopting a generational perspective with respect to social continuities and change and of locating childhood within such a life-course perspective. To this end she advocates the collection of further large-scale data sets through the use of quantitative methods developed specifically for children. These two kinds of approaches are important for describing the structural relationships which shape the forms that childhood takes in different societies across time and thus are also part of the phenomena which Jenks and Hendricks work with to account for the different discourse and social cultural processes through which children's everyday lives unfold.

Childhood and Children

If historical sources are to be used properly, we have to be clear as to our objectives: are we trying to write about childhood or children, and what issues does the distinction raise in relation to identification and interpretation? It is commonplace to define childhood, in a socio-historical context, as a structural feature of society – with its own social space – which largely determines the experiences of children, or at least shapes their commonality (Qvortrup et al. 1994; James et al. 1998; Corsaro 1997). Generally speaking, 'age', as a category, is *the* distinguishing criterion for identifying childhood, despite the influences on its meaning of class, gender and historical period (Jordanova 1989: 5). At any one time, throughout society there is usually a dominant overarching notion of 'childhood', albeit one that encompasses a variety of perceptions. As will be shown, historians have tended to focus on the *concept* of childhood rather than on the lives of children. This is not surprising since the former involves fewer methodological posers than the latter. But perhaps it also reflects adult interest in defining age groups so that generational matters may be effectively ordered.

It is worth noting, however, exactly what purpose childhood, as a 'unitary structural phenomenon' (James et al. 1998: 135), serves *vis-à-vis* meanings and understandings. I mean here that 'childhood' tends to conceal a range of birth points, many of which are at odds with one another in terms of capabilities, needs, vulnerability, knowledge and so on. Similarly 'children' are often referred to as if they were an undifferentiated collective. Yet in common speech we normally fragment childhood (and children) into a number of different identities: babies, toddlers, nursery children, juniors, secondary school pupils and young adolescents; alternatively, we may use categories favoured by psychologists: 'infants', 'young children', 'middle childhood' and 'pre and early adolescence' (Levine 1998: 102–31). This vocabulary permits us to insert 'children' into prescribed serial places. To record these dissimilarities is not to lapse into the 'stages' approach of conservative developmental psychology (James et al. 1998: 173–4), rather it is to recognize the different degrees of competence hidden within childhood which does, after all, involve 'a complex sequence of transitions' (Magnusson 1995: 300). In an ideal world, each transition would receive individual historical examination, though within the realm of childhood as a structural form. Unfortunately, in practice, they are thoughtlessly lumped together into a mêlée of age generalizations, resulting in flawed analyses. All this suggests that there is something of a tension, or perhaps it is a duplicity of meaning, between the nouns *childhood* and *children*. The former often assumes the latter without our knowing how or why. We need to remember such ambiguity (or is it ambivalence) in our reading, our research and our writing.

When we look at children, we are not looking at an idea but at *people* who, in many respects, cannot but be active in history, if only in the sense of how they deal with their daily situations (James et al. 1998: 78, 138; Corsaro 1997: 18). However, in the past, the majority of historians have had little explicit intellectual sympathy for children. Indeed (as will be shown), there are those who doubt that children can have a history; they argue that we can only ever understand childhood as a *cultural* construction. Such a view, if it were correct, would leave real, live children to the ethnographers. This discussion offers a more optimistic prognosis.

My basic premise is twofold: children are social actors and informants in their own right and childhood is a structural feature of all societies; it is not merely the early period of the life course (Hardman 1973; James 1998; Qvortrup et al. 1994). With this in mind, it should be understood that producing the history of children involves far more than the identification and interpretation of sources available for different historical periods. It is also necessary to practise theorizing childhood in order to see the interplay between 'childhood' as a concept and its place in the process of social theory. Of equal importance, if not more so, recognition has to be given to the fact that historians adopt what are in effect ideological positions with respect to age relations involving children. On this point, post-modernists are correct when they claim that historians are not outside the 'ideological fray' (Jenkins 1991: 20). Where history is concerned, then, sources are only one problem among many others. The crucial matter concerns the politics of age relations, which is instructed by adultism (Alanen 1992: 59),[1] meaning, in this regard, a view of children as naturally 'less' than adults in so far as they are in a state of becoming (adults), rather than being seen as complete and identifiable persons. Consequently, in much of the published work to date, children have been denied both a voice and, an essential feature of human identity, a rational standpoint.

The Historiographical Tradition

It is only since the 1960s that anything like a history of children and childhood has begun to emerge.[2] It was the well-documented publication of Ariès's *Centuries of Childhood* (English translation 1962), and the emergence of the 'new' social history in the late 1960s and early 1970s, that made the study of the family a popular research topic and gave rise to several controversies, some of which involved children. Ariès initiated a debate about childhood, rather than children, claiming that as an idea it was subject to historical change. He was especially interested in the development of the relationship between meanings and relations of childhood and the evolution of the family, arguing that since the seventeenth century the former had become the focus of the latter. For him the crucial influence was the emergence of the school as an age-graded institution, which segregated children

4   Macroanalysis of Childhood

Jens Qvortrup

> When I look back on my childhood I wonder how I survived at all. It was, of course, a miserable childhood: the happy childhood is hardly worth your while. Worse than the ordinary miserable childhood is the miserable Irish childhood, and worse yet is the miserable Irish Catholic childhood. People everywhere brag and whimper about the woes of their early years, but nothing can compare with the Irish version: the poverty; the shiftless loquacious alcoholic father; the pious defeated mother moaning by the fire; the English and the terrible things they did to us for eight hundred long years. Above all – we were wet.
>
> (McCourt 1997: 9)

Introduction

What Frank McCourt is saying on the very first page of *Angela's Ashes* is that Irish childhood was a wet childhood. He was probably wrong. I feel pretty sure that many sociologists and anthropologists would immediately present to him a sample of children who were not wet, only half wet, or merely wet during the night. Yet, McCourt gives us an impression of Irish childhood, which is quintessentially real: its Irish-ness, its Catholic-ness, miserable-ness, and above all, its wet-ness. Although not applicable for each and every child in Ireland, it conveys a picture which is recognizable of Irish children at the time and which achieved its distinction in comparison with childhoods in other countries; no one other childhood possessed this combination. Were any other childhoods wet? If so, no others were Catholic and wet, and for sure not Irish and Catholic and wet. Though McCourt did not think of it, he is actually using a particular method for coming to terms with his childhood, indirectly comparing it with other childhoods so as to make it as distinct as possible.

His methods, if one may use such a clinical term, for coming to this insight, probably come close to the comparative method of analysis. We would not have become wiser if he had not had the courage to generalize his insight. No one – besides himself and his many siblings – had such a childhood, but nevertheless he dared to abstract from these particularities to reach his conclusion about a miserable childhood which was Irish, Catholic and – above all – wet; had he pondered upon his childhood's particularity his book would still have been entertaining and moving, but we would not have been as wise.

It is sometimes suggested by researchers that it is dangerous to generalize, because we lose information; this is indeed true, but, I would suggest, losing information in a controlled way is the very idea of research. It was never the task of researchers to tell everything they knew; on the contrary, the task was always to sort out the most important features and findings, and one crucial criterion is to meet the demand for commonality. If this is not met, one fails to be able to classify – and what cannot be classified according to selected research problems, we should leave on our shelves as impressionistic memories.

Generalized insight presupposes causal factors; McCourt is – perhaps unwittingly – giving us them as well: nationality, religion, alcoholism, poverty, history and geo-politics – perhaps even pious defeated mothers. These were the factors that constructed Irish childhood. They have not been subjected to scientific scrutiny, and researchers might have chosen others, but this is not the point. The point is, once again, the method, which in principle is a correct one. Researchers must look for boundaries within which similarities are exceeding differences and through that locate those parameters which have explanatory value.

From my vantage point, as one with experience of a large-scale international and comparative project – Childhood as a Social Phenomenon – the trend in the new paradigm for the social studies of childhood seems, however, to have been drifting towards a micro-orientation,[1] following Prout and James' recommendation that

> Ethnography is a particularly useful methodology for the study of childhood. It allows children a more direct voice and participation in the production of sociological data than is usually possible through experimental or survey styles of research.
>
> (Prout and James 1990: 8–9 and unchanged in 1997: 8)

This is, indeed, an important methodology, provided one has the courage to generalize from the cases collected; to this end we need as many cases with as much information as possible. I am however more reluctant to accept their thesis if any prioritizing of methodologies is intended for there are many ways of collecting information about children's lives and childhood. No one method alone can produce all knowledge needed. In fact, much of the insight we have about children we have from sources in which children of flesh and blood are conspicuously distant, such as statistics collected at an aggregate level. Moreover, we are often forced to make inferences from knowledge about apparently childhood-alien topics in order to learn about children's life worlds. This is mostly the case, when we are mapping the life conditions of adults or political, economic, social and cultural realms in general. These are the realms, I suggest, which more than any others are forming and forging childhoods; they are largely independent variables as far as childhood in a given national context is concerned, but are due themselves to variation in an historical or intercultural comparative perspective.

I do not find it particularly useful to argue about the preponderance of either material or cultural factors; at the end of the day, both are structural factors, the former unequivocally so, the latter will enjoy the same status as they eventually achieve hegemonic influence, and both are subjected to secular changes. Which are the more or less influential in contributing to the architecture of childhood nobody knows. The point is that no child can evade the impact of economic or spatial forces, nor ideologies about children and the family – let alone political and economic ideologies and realities (see Davis, Watson and Cunningham-Burley, Chapter 10). Discussions of either structure or agency seem similarly abortive. Children are of course actors in a diversity of arenas, even where this is not visible to the ethnographic gaze; yet, they are born into economic and cultural circumstances which cannot be explained away. The overwhelming majority of Irish children – to refer for a last time to McCourt – could not help being impacted by religion and poverty and nationality, the latter imprinted by century-long traumatic experiences with a mighty neighbouring nation, whose children, *grosso modo*, obviously had other experiences.

The purpose of this chapter is therefore to explore the variability of childhood as a macro-phenomenon. As such, childhood is a variable, the contours of which are determined by an ensemble of parameters pertaining to a given society or any other macro-units 'defined as all those units the majority of whose *consequences* affect one or more societies, their combinations, or their sub-units' (Etzioni 1968: 49, my italics). This ensemble of parameters is what John Stuart Mill (1950: 211) in his comparative methodology calls an *instance* within which the *phenomenon* – e.g. childhood does or does not occur, or according to which it assumes more or less distinct values compared with other instances. While taking a dialectical relationship between instances and phenomena for granted, it is assumed that the 'instance' stands in a supra-sub relationship to the 'phenomenon', that in other words, we are dealing with a hierarchical relationship, theoretically speaking (Qvortrup 1989: 19).

What *is* important for macro-analysis, thus, is to look for strong explanatory instances; society, mode of production, culture, or – more vaguely – historical periods are such instances, while the phenomenon may be any kind of sub-unit *vis-à-vis* this instance. As abstractions (a necessary ingredient of comparative methodology), they are too crude to explain everything, but they do empirically influence phenomena such as education, wealth, health, housing, institutionalization, urbanization.[2] The instances mentioned are explanatorily strong in that they enable us to make predictions with a high degree of certainty; as supra-units they impose on their sub-units limits which can only at pains be transgressed by individuals. Industrialization, for example, has formed a new architecture of life conditions compared with the general life circumstances preceeding it; it has influenced not merely the most basic survival phenomena and indicators, but a whole framework of life.

There is no doubt that such variables – whatever their weight relative to each other – have played a part historically in producing the kind of society we know in the western world today. Basically, these variables have only exceptionally been invented or developed with any view to producing childhood(s); indeed, children themselves were hardly allotted any role as agents in inaugurating modernity, although to some extent they have been the objects of thoughts and plans and instrumentalized for safeguarding the wealth and prosperity of these countries' futures (de Lone 1979) or for embodying parents' own pasts and futures (Jenks 1996: 97pp; Beck 1986: 193). Finally, the interaction of any variables, which were brought into play, has not infrequently produced unintended consequences as powerful as those which have been planned for.

However, which of the *instances* or elements of modernity has been most influential in changing the *phenomenon* of childhood historically is of less importance for my argument than the assumption that it has been historically altered and formed in accordance with the demands of prevailing instances. Ariès's (1962) proposition that childhood was a cultural invention is important in the sense that it suggests a non-incidental modality in the shape of childhood due to the changing requirements of society. The importance of his study was its ability to make intelligible a historical change in both the architecture of and the attitudes towards childhood, while rendering its diversification due to time and place relatively immaterial. Thus he seems to concur with Bloch's methodological statement that 'the unity of place is only disorder; only the unity of problem makes a center' (Bloch 1934: 81; translated and quoted in Skocpol 1994: 89).

Of the numerous possibilities to demonstrate the power of macro-conditions in producing childhoods and thus children's life worlds, I shall select merely three, which necessarily involve comparisons, historically and interculturally, between countries and between generations. The last differs from the former two in that it applies most conveniently (although not by way of principle) to intra-societal relations.

among others Marc Bloch and Fernand Braudel belonged. The latter contended that it was at the '"microscopical" level that one hopes to perceive structural laws of the most general kind' (Braudel 1972: 33). The programme of the Annales school was to create the long view in history on the basis of minute studies of daily life, but this could not be done without the ever present reality of the macro-world. The intersection of the micro-events and the macro-perspective is what Braudel calls a conjuncture, which is the point at which we must finally arrive.

> In my view, [he explains] research must constantly move between social reality and the model, in a succession of readjustments and journeys ever patiently reviewed. Thus the model is both an attempt to explain a given structure, and an instrument with which one can examine it, and compare it, and test its solidity and its very life. If I constructed a model, starting from contemporary reality, I should want to locate it at once in reality, then make it move back over time, right to its birth, if possible. After that I should calculate its probable life-span as far as its next breaking point according to the concomitant movement of other social realities. In other ways, using it as an element of comparison, I can move it through time and space in search of other realities capable of being illuminated by it.
>
> (Braudel 1972: 33)

Experience shows that there are no good reasons to argue about the paramouncy of either a micro- or macro-level approach; neither is it demanded that each and everybody must in his or her research capture all levels. The choice is partly made by inclination and/or temperament. In the end it is nonetheless a requirement that our research problem – childhood – be seen from as many fruitful angles as possible.

My inclination is towards elucidating structures of childhood – be they economic, social, political or ideological; these constitute frameworks that cannot be discounted, their salience and their being made intelligible depending on the insight they provide into children's everyday life. This means among other things that insight from one level must not contradict insight from another level within any chosen instance.

One way of reaching this goal is by using a comparative methodology in the sense of crossing boundaries between what Mill (1950) called instances, because it enables us to see realities which otherwise remain opaque, because we are too close to our research object; if the new social studies of childhood does not meet the challenge of dialectically connecting – in a conjuncture – different levels of reality, it will hardly come of age, become a household member of the scientific community or be seen as useful for understanding and possibly changing realities of childhood(s).

93

Krüsselberg, H-G. (1987) 'Vital capital policy and the unity of the social budget: economic prospects of a social policy for childhood', in The Sociology of Childhood, special issue ed. by J. Qvortrup of *International Journal of Sociology* 81–97.

Lone, R. de (1979) *Small Futures: Children, Inequality, and the Limits of Liberal Reform*, New York and London: Harcourt Brace Jovanovich.

McCourt, F. (1997) *Angela's Ashes*, New York: Simon and Schuster.

Matthews, H. (1998) 'The right to be outdoors', *Family Policy Bulletin*, summer.

Mill, J.S. (1950) *Philosophy of Scientific Method*, New York: Hafner.

Nauck, B. (1995) 'Kinder als Gegenstand der Sozialberichterstattung – Konzepte, Methoden und Befunde im Überblick', in B. Nauck and H. Bertram (eds) *Kinder in Deutschland: Lebensverhältnisse von Kindern im Regionalvergleich*, Deutsche Jugend Institut Familien-Survey 5. Opladen: Leske and Budrich.

Oldman, D. (1991) 'Conflict and accommodation between ideologies in the regulation of children's rights', Paper to the Conference on Social Policies for Children and Adolescents, Florence, printed as 'I diritti del bambino: conflitto e compromesso tra ideologie', in *Politiche Sociali Per l'Infanzia e l'Adolescenza*, Milano: Edizioni Unicopli.

Preston, S.H. (1984) 'Children and the elderly: divergent paths for America's dependents', *Demography* 21: 435–57.

Prout, A. and James, A. ([1990] 1997) 'A new paradigm for the sociology of childhood? Provenance, promise and problems', in A. James and A. Prout (eds) *Constructing and Reconstructing Childhood. Contemporary Issues in the Sociological Study of Childhood*, 2nd edn, London: Falmer Press.

Qvortrup, J. (1987) 'Introduction', in The Sociology of Childhood, special issue ed. by J. Qvortrup of *International Journal of Sociology* 17(3): 3–37.

Qvortrup, J. (1989) 'Comparative research and its problems', in K. Boh et al. (eds) *Changing Patterns of European Family Life: A Comparative Analysis of 14 European Countries*, London and New York: Routledge.

Qvortrup, J. (ed.) (1993) *Childhood as a Social Phenomenon: Lessons from an International Project*, Eurosocial Report 47, Vienna: European Centre.

Qvortrup, J., Bardy, M., Sgritta, G. and Wintersberger H. (eds) (1994) *Childhood Matters: Social Theory, Practice and Politics*, Aldershot: Avebury.

Rainwater, L. and Smeeding, T.M. (1995) *Doing Poorly: The Real Income of American Children in a Comparative Perspective*, Luxembourg Income Study working paper no. 127.

Ringen, S. (1997) *Citizens, Families, and Reform*, Oxford: Clarendon Press.

Salmi, M. (1995a) 'Depression och barn [Depression and children]', Paper to Eighth Nordic Seminar on Social Policy, Hässelby, Stockholm, February.

Salmi, M. (1995b) 'Barn i den ekonomiska depressionen [Children in the economic depression]', Paper to Eighteenth Nordic Congress of Sociology, Helsinki, June.

Sgritta, G.B. (1997) 'Inconsistencies: childhood on the economic and political agenda', *Childhood* 4(4): 375–404.

Sgritta, G. and Saporiti, A. (1990) *Childhood as a Social Phenomenon: National Report Italy*, Eurosocial Report 36/2, Vienna: European Centre.

Skocpol, T. (1994) *Social Revolutions in the Modern World*, Cambridge: Cambridge University Press.

Smith, J.P. (1989) 'Children among the poor', *Demography* May (2): 235–48.

Stephens, J.D. and Huber, E. (1995) 'The Welfare State in hard times', Paper to Conference on Politics and Political Economy of Contemporary Capitalism, Humboldt University and the Wissenschaftszentrum, Berlin, May.

Thomas, W.I. (ed.) (1966) *On the Social Organisation and Social Personality*, Chicago: University of Chicago Press.

Thomson, D. (1996) *Selfish Generations? How Welfare States Grow Old*, Cambridge: White Horse Press.

Unicef (1997) *The State of the World's Children*, Oxford: Oxford University Press for Unicef.

Ward, C. (1994) 'Opportunities for childhoods in the late twentieth century Britain', B. Mayall (ed.) in *Children's Childhoods: Observed and Experienced*, London: Falmer Press.

Wintersberger, H. (1997) 'Children and the welfare mix: distributive justice between generations in a welfare society', Paper based on lecture given at the South Jutland University Centre, 9. January.

Wirth, L. (1945) 'The problem of minority groups', in R. Linton (ed.) *The Science of Man in the World Crisis*, New York: Columbia University Press.

Wolfenstein, M. (1955) 'Fun morality: an analysis of recent American childtraining literature', in M. Mead and M. Wolfenstein (eds) *Childhood in Contemporary Cultures*, Chicago and London: University of Chicago Press.

Zeiher, H.J. and Zeiher, H. (1994) *Orte und Zeiten der Kinder: Soziales Leben im Alltag von Großtadtkindern*, Weinheim: Juventa Verlag.

Zinnecker, J. (1990) 'Vom Straßenkind zum verhäuslichten Kind: Kindheitsgeschichte im Proze der Zivilization'. in I. Behnken (ed.) *Stadtgesellschaft und Kindheit im Proze der Zivilization: Konfigurationen städtischer Lebensweise zu Beginn des 20. Jahrhunderts*, Opladen: Leske and Budrich.

5 Children as Respondents

The Challenge for Quantitative Methods

Jacqueline Scott

Introduction

The sentiment that children should be seen and not heard could not be more inappropriate for the current era in which there is a growing demand for research that involves interviewing children. The construction of childhood that views children as incomplete adults is coming under attack and there is a new demand for research that focuses on children as actors in their own right. The French historian Philip Ariès (1962) suggested that modern western childhood is unique in the way that it quarantines children from the world of adults, so that childhood is associated with play and education rather than work and economic responsibility. The quarantine of childhood is represented in the exclusion of children from statistics and other social accounts (Qvortrup 1990) and there exists very little material that directly addresses the experience of childhood, at the societal level. (For a useful overview of quantitative data available on children in Britain, see Church and Summerfield 1997.) In surveys of the general population, children have been usually regarded as out of scope and samples are usually drawn from the adult population, with a minimum age of 16 or 18. Interviews with children have long been central to the research of developmental psychologists, child psychiatrists and educational specialists, but until quite recently general purpose surveys have not included children as respondents (see Roberts, Chapter 11).

In this chapter I reflect on why children are so often excluded from large-scale quantitative research. I argue that the social and economic questions that such research addresses are often framed in ways where the adultcentric bias is unacknowledged and inappropriate. I also elaborate on how, at least for research using the life course perspective (Elder et al. 1993; Elder 1995), the crucial concepts of choice and agency means that it is essential to collect information from children themselves concerning their present experiences and future aspirations. Until recently survey researchers, when investigating aspects of childhood, have preferred to ask adult respondents such as parents or teachers to report on children's lives, rather than to ask children themselves. In part, this has been because of concerns about the cognitive ability of children to process and respond to structured questions about behaviour, perceptions, opinions and beliefs. Drawing on research from cognitive psychology, I suggest ways that questionnaires and interview practice can be modified to make them more suitable for young respondents. I also reflect on ways that practical and ethical challenges posed by the inclusion of children in general surveys can be overcome. By including children in population surveys, especially longitudinal surveys, social scientists can improve the theoretical understanding and empirical knowledge of the dynamics of social inclusion and exclusion that are so evident in childhood experiences and life course trajectories.

The Exclusion of Children from Social Surveys

Survey practice has tended to follow the 'quarantine' approach with children being, at best, the subject of proxy information and, at worst, invisible. Moreover, much of the research that does take children into account is concerned with the impact of children on adult lives, rather than focusing on children as social actors in their own right. Panel studies of households, for example, are conducted as if children are auxiliary members, whose presence contributes to measures of household size, density, the labour market participation of mothers, household income and the like. Survey research that is interested in children *per se* is relatively rare. Yet, as any parent will attest, children do have voices, they express opinions, they observe and judge, and they exert a crucial influence on the way families and households function. Moreover, there is often a very large gulf between parental observations about their child and the child's own perceptions. For example, when asked about their children's subjective health, parents portray a much rosier picture of children's well-being than children do of themselves (Scott 1997a). Furthermore, adolescents may go out of their way to conceal risky behaviours that would invoke parental sanctions or concern. Of course there are topics where the responsible parent is better placed to provide information about the child than the child themselves, for example health diagnosis that relies on detailed knowledge of early childhood illness. Nevertheless, for questions tapping the child's own viewpoint, proxy information is clearly inadequate.

In this chapter I argue that the best people to provide information on the child's perspective, actions and attitudes are children themselves. Children provide reliable responses if questioned about events that are meaningful to their lives. For example, in investigations of latch-key children, researchers have found that accounts by parents and children often differ. Moreover, children have provided crucial insights into the diverse ways that young people appraise and respond to situations where they are left unsupervised

(Solberg 1990; Belle et al. 1997). Similarly, research on children whose parents divorce has reached the point where children's views are crucial for examining the risk factors associated with the diverse ways in which marital disruption can affect children's development (Elliot and Richards 1991; Kiernan 1992). Previous studies have usually focused on aggregate associations (e.g. divorce and children's lower educational attainment) but, with children's own accounts and insights, it is possible to examine how some young people's aspirations and priorities prove resilient to the most disadvantaged family circumstances (Furstenberg and Hughes 1995).

The quantitative data we collect about society becomes far richer if our accounts include information that can be provided by children. Once children are viewed as competent social actors in their own right then it clearly makes sense to ask them about their own contributions and participation in social and economic life. The range of questions that it is appropriate to ask children is much wider than was previously believed. For example, it has been standard practice for definitions of work to be confined to adult activity that failed to include the child's own work contributions (Morrow 1994). Yet, children's ability to perform household chores and care for younger siblings can be crucial to the household economy, when both parents are out at work (Solberg 1990). Similarly, time budget studies often ignored the fact that children have their own time (for an exception, see Timmer et al. 1985). Even studies on the costs of children have tended to view children as items on the parent's budget, rather than as economic actors who exercise considerable clout in family expenditure on food and consumer durables. Including children as respondents can, therefore, improve our knowledge on a whole range of social and economic issues by providing a more accurate and complete account of social life.

Yet interviewing children does pose some particular practical and methodological problems and the current state of knowledge about conducting survey interviews with children is very fragmented. There are many problems to be solved when the respondents are children, including problems of language use, literacy and different stages of cognitive development. There is also a heightened concern about data quality, with some scepticism about whether an adult interviewer can obtain reliable and valid accounts from children, especially in areas where the information may be sensitive and subject to adult sanctions and control. In addition, issues of confidentiality and ethics become especially important when interviewing minors. Yet, as this chapter shows, there are solutions to such problems that deserve consideration, given the potential benefits of collecting data directly from children themselves.

In this chapter, I discuss some of the accumulated knowledge regarding the techniques for interviewing children in person in large-scale surveys and the strategies for optimizing the measures used and the quality of the resulting data. The chapter draws together practical knowledge from diverse sources and reflects on the lessons that can be learned for quantitative research concerning children. This practical knowledge comes from a very wide range of disciplines, including psychology, anthropology, education, criminology and sociology. In addition, in order to illustrate the constraints and practical challenges of including children in an ongoing large-scale, general purpose, survey, I describe, as a case study, the development and implementation of a Young Person's questionnaire for children aged 11–15 in the British Household Panel Study. First, however, I consider why, in our supposedly child-oriented society, children are so often ignored by large-scale, general population, survey research.

The exclusion of children in surveys has at least four distinct causes. First, there is the inertia of practice. Most studies, even when their subject matter requires information about children, interview only adult respondents. Second, children may be omitted because of the tendency to accredit adults with greater knowledge, experience and power (Backett and Alexander 1991). Third, interviewing children is viewed as too problematic to be worth the possible pay off. Interviewing minors poses both practical and ethical issues which researchers might wish to avoid. The fourth reason is ignorance or perhaps a half-truth. Children are commonly believed to lack the communication, cognitive and social skills that are the prerequisite of good respondents. Experimental research has clearly demonstrated that even preschool children are able to appreciate someone else's point of view, can make social judgements and even identify false intentions and beliefs (Astington et al. 1988). Nevertheless, children's cognitive capacity clearly does increase with age and the rudimentary levels of cognitive development remain relevant for understanding the question and answer process and for highlighting the ways in which children may differ from adult respondents.

Different Methods for Different Age Groups

Research methods that involve children as respondents have to take account of the wide range of cognitive and social development that depends primarily on age, but also on the gender, socio-economic background, and ethnicity of the child. Standard questionnaire techniques are clearly inappropriate with preschool children. For example, very young children find it difficult to distinguish between what is said and what is meant and thus almost any hypothetical question becomes problematic (Robinson 1986). This implies that less structured methods of interviewing are more appropriate for younger children (see Mayall, Chapter 6). However, once children have reached the age of 7, it is possible to use both individual and group semi-structured interviews with children. The classic study *The Lore and Language of Schoolchildren* involved interviews with more than 5,000 children (from 7 to early teens) and revealed a distinctive child-centred culture of customs and beliefs (Opie and Opie 1959). One problem is that while pre-teen children can and do tell us about themselves, they have also mastered the art of impression management and, like adults, will tend to edit their answers (Fine and Sandstrom 1988). Thus the Opies found that if they asked about superstitions, children said (as they are expected to say) that all superstitions are silly. But probing the child's own perspective revealed a world of half-beliefs and superstitious practices that invest children with some degree of control over the unpredictability of everyday experiences.

Thus, once children have reached the age where they are able to process and respond to standard questions, they are also adept at controlling what they reveal. This is aptly illustrated by a study of children aged seven onwards to investigate the strategies used to persuade parents and other adults to buy them things (Middleton et al. 1994). Using group discussions in school, the researchers found that children reported using begging, repetition, direct action, bribery, part-payment, negotiation, threats and actions, each with varying degrees of success. The range of techniques reported by 7–8 year olds was already large and not much was added to the persuasion repertoire, after the age of 11. The authors note that, if anything, the younger children were less reticent in discussion than teenagers. By adolescence, young people are wary of revealing their secrets to an adult.

For children under 11, visual stimuli can be especially useful in the questioning process, because pictures make the issue far more concrete than verbal representation alone (see O'Kane, Chapter 7, and Christensen and James, Chapter 8). Aids to memory can also be used to good effect, as children tend to forget even a relatively limited set of response options. Often a simple modification of question format is sufficient. For example the standard Likert type response (agree strongly, agree, neither agree nor disagree, disagree strongly) can easily be unfolded by first asking 'Do you agree or disagree?' and then probing for strength of feeling. Children's performance on memory tasks improves markedly with age and, by 11, children's ability to remember is not so different from adults (although the information content of memory is much more limited). Most children of 11 and older are fully able to articulate their perceptions, opinions and beliefs and, with relatively little adaptation, surveys designed for adults can be used with adolescents.

Although, by adolescence (aged 11 onwards), it is possible to use a standardized questionnaire instrument, problems of literacy, confidentiality and context have to be taken into account. Often the instruments are very similar to the ones used with adults and, with adult help, standardized instruments can be successfully used with even younger children. In order to identify problems with comprehension and ambiguities in question wording, to detect flippancy and boredom, and to discover discrepancies between the children's understanding and the researcher's intent, pretesting the survey instrument is crucial. A variety of pretest methods can be useful, including cognitive techniques such as asking the child to 'think aloud', coding of non-verbal behaviours, and even video analysis of the interview interactions. Certainly, most questionnaires developed for adults or older children will need some adaptation before they are suitable to use with younger children.

It is also sometimes necessary to adapt standard interview practice. For example, interviewers may need more leeway than is normal, as children tend to ask for more guidance than adults, especially when they are unsure what a question means. In such circumstances, it is preferable for interviewers to paraphrase the question, than give the standard response whatever it means to you. Standard interview practice might also have to be modified to protect children's privacy and confidentiality, especially in settings where children are likely to worry about their responses being reported to the adult authorities. Unfortunately, confidentiality issues can also become real ethical dilemmas if children reveal self-actions or adult behaviours that put them at risk (Stanley and Sieber 1992).

Table 5.1 presents, by way of illustration, summary information for seven large-scale social surveys that collect information from children using structured questionnaires, in Britain. The different surveys have different strengths and weaknesses, depending on the context and method used, as I discuss below.

The Importance of Context in Interviewing Children

Children's social worlds span many different settings but home and school are two of the most important (see Mayall, Chapter 6). Context is especially important in interviewing children because the expression of the child's personality, in terms of behaviour and attitudinal preferences, is often so context dependent. The same child could be boisterous and outspoken at home, but shy and reserved at school. Thus *where* the interviews are carried out is quite likely to influence the *way* children respond. In addition, the interviewer setting is important because the social meaning children will attach to concepts such as work or honesty may differ depending on whether children are at home or at school. The mode of interview is also very important in terms of data quality. Whether the interview is face to face, by telephone or self-completion may enhance or reduce the likelihood of different response biases such as social desirability or response contamination. (These and other response biases are discussed more fully in the next section.)

Interviewing children in schools is, on the whole, more cost-effective than interviewing children in the home. One problem of classroom surveys is that they usually rely on self-completion schedules, which can encounter difficulties with literacy and motivation. Motivation is often less of a problem with younger children, who may even approach a survey questionnaire as

Table 5.1 Surveys interviewing children in Britain

Study name and survey type	Country and year	Sample	Method of data collection	Context
British Household Panel Study	Britain 1994– annual	Children aged 11–15 in panel households $N \approx 900$	Walkman tape self-administered	Home interview
British Social Attitudes	Britain 1994	Children aged 12–19 $N = 580$	Face-to-face	Home interview
National Child Development Study Longitudinal Cohort	Britain 1965, 1969, 1974, 1981, 1991	Children born in one week of 1958 $N \approx 16,000$	Face-to-face	Home interview
Twenty-07 Longitudinal Cohort	West Scotland 1987/8	Youngest cohort aged 15 $N \approx 1,000$	Face-to-face and self-completion	Home interview
National Crime Survey	England and Wales 1992	Childred aged 12–15 $N \approx 1,000$	Self-completion	Home interview
OPCS Smoking Survey	England 1994	School children $N = 3,045$	Self-completion and smoking diary	School interview
School Health Education Unit, University of Exeter	England 1984– annual	School children aged 11–16 $N \approx 10,000$	Self-completion	School interview

if it were a test. This test-taking mentality, although likely to enhance what is perceived to be the correct response, may be beneficial in making children pay greater attention to the questions. A main drawback of school-based interviewing is that children of all ages are likely to be influenced by the proximity of class mates. Even if answers are supposedly confidential, children are likely to quiz one another on their responses and may be tempted to give answers that win favour with the peer-group.

Interviewing children in the home is more time consuming and therefore more costly. One concern that is usual in contacting children at home is the need to deal with parents as gatekeepers. In my experience, with the British Household Panel Study (BHPS), this rarely caused a problem, but parents were already participating in the survey. On the whole, we found that children are very keen to participate and seem pleased to be treated as household members who have something useful to contribute in their own right. Interviewing children, if anything, improved our household response rates because their enthusiasm raised the interest of other household members. With household studies, there is the risk, however, that children's answers will be influenced by the presence of parents or siblings. Even if the interviewer is instructed to interview the child in private if possible, complete privacy is often impractical or elusive in the home. In a later section, I discuss how we overcame the privacy and confidentiality issues in the BHPS Young Person's Survey.

Interviews with children at home are usually carried out in person and this has at least three advantages over the self-completion methods that are often used in schools. First, it is possible to include more complex routing so that particular questions are only asked in specific circumstances that have been elicited by earlier responses. Different questions, for example, might be appropriate depending on whether the child lives with one parent or with two. Second, it is possible to make use of visual aids and show cards which allow for more elaborate response options. Third, if the questions do not elicit sufficiently clear or elaborate responses then the interviewer is able to prompt for further information. All three are particularly important when interviewing young adolescents. Routing is needed to ensure that children at different stages of social development are asked appropriate questions. Visual aids are useful when there are vocabulary problems and limited attention span. Interviewer prompts are essential when inadequate answers are given, because of lack of communication skills.

New interviewing techniques using Computer Assisted Personal Interviewing (CAPI) methods add further enhancements that could be used to good effect with younger respondents. Not only do they make complex routing relatively effortless for the interviewer, but also they provide the opportunity to incorporate videos and other visual and audio stimuli that reduce the need to rely so heavily on verbal questions and answers.

Telephone interviewing can be a far more economical alternative and, at least in the USA has proved effective with children aged 11 and older (Reich and Earls 1990). The success of interviewing young people by telephone is not surprising given the amount of time teenagers spend on the phone confiding in friends. But a major drawback with the telephone interview is the possible lack of privacy. This is particularly crucial when interviewing children and may limit the usefulness of telephone interviews as a means of collecting sensitive information.

One relatively novel method of collecting sensitive information from children is the diary method. Diaries are also good for collecting information that is too detailed for retrospective reports to be reliable. In principle, the method should be useful if the format can be made sufficiently simple and internal checks for accuracy can be devised. The Family Expenditure Survey, for example, has incorporated expenditure diaries that are used with children (Jarvis 1994) and the new panel study Home On-Line is using a time-use diary with children aged 9–15 (BHPS 1998).

Are Children any less Reliable than Adult Respondents?

An old proverb says it is only children and fools who tell the truth. In contrast, Belloc's cautionary tales tell us of Matilda who told such dreadful lies it made us gasp and stretch one's eyes. Social constructions include the contradictory portrayal of childhood as a time of wide-eyed innocence and wilful deceit. In this section, three questions will be considered. First, are children any more or less reliable than adult respondents? Second, how can we evaluate the quality of data from children? Third, how can we improve data quality?

There is a seeming reluctance to take children's responses at face value, perhaps because children's opinions are seen as especially pliable and susceptible to suggestion. This is an area that is coming under the glare of public scrutiny in recent times, as there is mounting concern about the reliability of children's testimonies in cases concerning child abuse and the like (Fincham et al. 1994; Ceci and Bruck 1994). There is little reason to discredit children as respondents, however, because in highly traumatic circumstances children, like adults, have been known to lie or display memory distortion. Moreover, modern psychological and medical evidence suggests that children are more reliable as witnesses than previously thought, and reliability can be increased by skilful interviewing (Spencer and Flin 1990). The interviewing advice is very familiar to survey researchers: give the child unambiguous and comprehensible instructions at the start of the interview; avoid leading questions; explicitly permit 'don't know' responses to avoid best guesses; and interview the child on home ground, if possible.

There is growing evidence to suggest that the best source of information about issues pertinent to children is the children themselves. While parents and teachers can provide useful insights into child behaviour, the direct interviewing of children provides a far more complete account of the child's life. For example, in the health domain, young children often report depressed symptoms of which their parents appear to be unaware and school-age children report far more fears than their mothers' accounts reveal (Tizard 1986). Older children may be involved with alcohol or drugs without their parents' knowledge. Yet, when it comes to younger children's own behavioural problems, parents can be more forthcoming than the children (Reich and Earls 1990). For many areas of research, therefore, it is desirable to gather information from multiple sources, as any one account may be biased (Tein et al. 1994).

Improving Data Quality

The quality of data that results from interviewing children will depend on a number of different factors. First and most basic is the appropriateness of the research topic and measures used. In designing suitable measures for young children, researchers have to, at minimum, ensure that the questions really do measure the desired concept; that the questions are unambiguous, and that children interpret the questions in the way the researcher intended. Research concerning the question and answer process in surveys with children is extremely sparse. However, the research clearly suggests that the clarity of questions influence the quality of the data, especially for younger children and that complex questions are problematic regardless of the child's age (De Leeuw and Otter 1995).

We also know that both younger children and adolescents alike tend to respond to adult questioning, whether or not they know the answer, or have an attitude on the issue at hand (Parker 1984; Weber et al. 1994). Children are often called on by adults to give answers even when they do not have the information and responses of 'don't know' can be deemed as cheek, inattention or lack of cooperation. It is understandable then if children are likely to construct a response rather than refuse to answer, but this can make for low stability on issues where the children's knowledge is limited or their attitudes are non-crystalized (Vaillancourt 1973). Thus in order to achieve meaningful data, questions have to be pertinent and relevant to the children's own experience or knowledge. However, when this condition is met it is clear that even quite young children can make insightful respondents, as the following two studies illustrate.

In the USA, a specially adapted self-report instrument measuring anti-social behaviour was administered to boys as young as 7 (Loeber and Farrington 1989). In order to obtain independent measures of behaviour, information was also collected from the primary parent or caretaker. When questioning the boys, interviewers first checked whether each item was clearly understood, by probing for examples. Only those items which the child could interpret were included in the subsequent inventory. Information was collected on whether the child had ever engaged in each kind of antisocial behaviour, and if so whether they had done so in the past six months. Bounded recall methods were used to establish the six month period, using Christmas, school terms and events from personal life.

Not surprisingly, there were marked differences between 7 year olds and 10 year olds in understanding the meaning of questions, with skipping school, for example, understood only by 75 per cent of American first-graders (aged 6–7) and almost 100 per cent of fourth-graders (aged 10–11). The most prevalent antisocial behaviour was hitting siblings (a concept well understood by all). The boys' estimates were fairly consistent with parental reports, but for most behaviours there was higher correlation between parental and child reports at age 7 than at age 10. One possible interpretation is that older children are less reliable. This, however, would be at odds with nearly all other empirical evidence, and a far more likely interpretation is that mothers know less about the behaviour of older children. Thus the different correlations reflect different states of parental knowledge.

In an Australian study of children in families, even primary school aged children (aged 8–9) were able to give articulate and informative responses to questions about objective family circumstances as long as the questions were about the here and now, or very recent past (Amato and Ochiltree 1987). However, this study provides clear evidence that questions that are outside the child's own experience, such as what parents do at work, are problematic if the interest is in adult job characteristics rather than children's perceptions. The objective quality of data, for this sort of question, improves markedly with older children (aged 15–16), who give answers that are more in line with the parental response.

Asking questions that are meaningful to the child's own experience is not, however, sufficient to guarantee that children will give meaningful answers. A second factor that is fundamental to improving data quality concerns the child's willingness and ability to answer the questions and articulate his or her subjective experience. This depends in part on the appropriateness, number and order of the response alternatives. One method of testing the effects of response alternatives is to use a split ballot whereby the sample is randomly split and a different version is given to each half. In a rare split ballot experiment with school children (aged 10 and over), evidence was found that children were prone to a primacy effect, being more likely to choose the option that appeared first when required to select among a list of five or more options (Hershey and Hill 1976). A similar problem occurred when using multi-item picture stimuli. Pictures are often considered useful because not only are they non-verbal but also they hold the limited attention of younger children. However, pictures do not ease the basic decision-making process and, when interviewing children, responses are likely to be less prone to measurement error if the choices are kept simple.

Children's responses will also be subject to the standard biases that have been relatively well researched in the question and answer process for adults – things like context effects, acquiescence bias, social desirability and the like. However, it is important not to simply assume that findings applicable to adults will generalize to children. For example, it has been claimed that children may be less susceptible than adults to social desirability bias. However, the validity of this claim depends on the definition of social desirability. Social desirability is often defined in adultcentric terms. For example, good citizenship tends to be interpreted in terms of voting, community participation and the like. There are standard devices for overcoming adult reluctance to report behaviours that contravene what is perceived as socially desirable and to answer threatening questions whether they be about alcohol consumption, infidelity or the like (see Bradburn and Sudburn 1979). There is less consensus on what counts as a threatening question for children because what counts as appropriate behaviour is age dependent. In addition, children's own ideas about social desirability are heavily context dependent. For example, in one situation children might be tempted to downplay their reports of delinquent behaviour and cigarette or drug use, but in another situation they may be prone to exaggeration.

It is also the case that context effects and acquiescence bias may well take a different form, at different stages of the life course, depending on the subject matter at issue. For example, the norm of reciprocity which exerts a powerful influence on adults to answer contiguous questions in an even-handed way (Schuman and Presser 1981) may not have the same moral imperative for younger children. However, it has been claimed that young children are particularly suggestible and interviewers approbation or disapproval can have a marked effect. Nevertheless, experimental work found little evidence of acquiescence bias among older school-aged children (Hershey and Hill 1976). This is an area where clearly more research is needed but, until we have more evidence, it seems good practice to include internal consistency checks, where possible, when interviewing children.

A third set of issues concerns the children's motivation to give careful and truthful answers. In this regard, the interviewer and the rapport between interviewer and child are crucial. A good relationship can encourage more forthcoming responses, especially when children are convinced that their responses are truly confidential. However, the interviewer and the relation between interviewer and child can also be a source of error. For instance, interviewers who are intimidating or impatient may inhibit children in a way that has damaging consequences for data quality. None of these factors are distinctive to children – they all apply to adult respondents as well – but

Jacqueline Scott

Thus, in order to ensure group identity and cohesion we separated the groups by gender, age (11–13 years and 13–15 years) and socio-economic category. The groups were conducted in three different parts of England: the South, the Midlands and the North. The recruiting and conduct of the focus groups was carried out by the qualitative division of NOP, which used a combination of doorstep screening and snow-balling to fulfil the recruitment criteria.

Group sessions were conducted in the interviewer's home. The children's focus groups lasted approximately two hours, with a break for a fast food snack at half-time. The group leader followed a detailed discussion guide, which included topics such as freedom and rules in the house, family communication and sources of advice, health beliefs and practices, anxiety and depression and future aspirations and expectations. For some of the topics visual materials were used to stimulate discussion (for example a picture of Munch's *The Scream* was used to probe feelings of anguish). In addition, some semi-structured questions were included that we hoped might prove suitable measures for this age group. For example we showed a card with a range of smiley faces to see whether young people could identify their state of happiness with respect to different aspects of life. We feared that the smiley faces might be insulting to children of this age range, who are so sensitive to being treated as kids. However, to our surprise, the scale worked extremely well, prompting some very sophisticated discussion of mood states and changes. Even children as young as 11 have remarkable insight into impression management and self-presentation in everyday life and drew attention to the fact that answers might be different depending on whether the question wanted to know how you feel inside, how you are trying to appear to other people, or how other people perceive you to be (Scott et al. 1995).

A further use of the focus groups was to inform the development of the Walkman method of interviewing. At the end of the focus groups, Walkmans were handed out to each participant together with a short self-completion booklet in which they could record their answers. This short test interview was designed to provide feedback on the voice type, the speed of questions delivery, and the clearest design for the answer booklet. It was also important to test out the appropriate format of questions and, in particular, whether children could handle open as well as closed questions in the taped interviews. Group discussion then gave more general feedback on the Walkman method. Fortunately young people are well familiar with Walkman sets and are able to manage well without adult intervention. The only technical problems were caused by adult ineptitude with the machines!

Feedback from these groups indicated that young people were very sensitive to the quality of the voice rather than having a preference for a particular sex, age, or accent. There was, however, less consensus about

6 By contrast a Finnish research colleague, Leena Alanen, has had no difficulty in securing consent from parents to her walking home with children from school, and going with them to the places where they spend their time after school. This general consent allows her to follow the children's lead, wherever they choose to take her.

7 As part of the Economic and Social Research Council's Children 5–16 Programme, two projects are studying children's use of space: Childhood, Urban Space and Citizenship, and Exploring the Fourth Environment.

8 A comprehensive discussion of measures needed to recognise children's rights is given in a report by the Children's Rights Development Unit (1994).

References

Children's Rights Development Unit (CRDU) (1994) *A UK Agenda for Children*, London: CRDU.

Corsaro, W. (1997) *The Sociology of Childhood*, Thousand Oaks, CA: Pine Forge Press.

James, A. (1996) 'Learning to be friends', *Childhood* 3(3): 313–30.

Kelley, P., Mayall, B. and Hood, S. (1997) 'Children's accounts of risk', *Childhood* 4(3): 305–24.

Mandell, N. (1991) 'The least-adult role in studying children', in F.C. Waksler (ed.) *Studying the Social Worlds of Children: Sociological Readings*, London: Falmer Press.

Mayall, B. (1994) *Negotiating Health: Children at Home and Primary School*. London: Cassell.

Mayall, B. (1996) *Children, Health and the Social Order*, Buckingham: Open University Press.

Mayall, B., Bendelow, G., Barker, S., Storey, P. and Veltman, M. (1996) *Children's Health in Primary Schools*, London: Falmer Press.

Moore, R.C. (1986) *Childhood's Domain: Play and Place in Child Development*, London: Croom Helm.

Qvortrup, J. (1994) 'Childhood matters: an introduction', in J. Qvortup, M. Bardy, G. Sgritta and H. Wintersberger (eds) *Childhood Matters: Social Theory, Practice and Politics*, Aldershot: Avebury.

Sgritta, G.B. (1997) 'Childhood on the economic and political agenda', *Childhood* 4(4): 375–404.

Therborn, G. (1996) 'Child politics', *Childhood* 3(1): 29–44.

Thorne, B. (1993) *Gender Play: Girls and Boys in School*, New Brunswick, NJ: Rutgers University Press.

Tizard, B. and Hughes, M. (1984) *Young Children Learning*, London: Fontana.

7 The Development of Participatory Techniques

Facilitating Children's Views about Decisions which Affect Them

Claire O'Kane

Introduction

Since the late 1980s there has been an increasing interest in listening to children's experiences and viewpoints, as separate to and different from their adult carers, an interest in line with the establishment of a new paradigm for the study of childhood, which seeks to explore childhood, children's relationships and cultures as areas of study in their own right (see James and Prout 1990). The emergence of the paradigm in part reflects a move away from seeing children as passive recipients of adult socialization, to a recognition that children are social actors in their own right, are active participants in the construction and determination of their experiences, other people's lives, and the societies in which they live.

The methodological shift in research methods, from approaches which view children as 'objects of concern' to methods which engage children as 'active participants' has been charted elsewhere (see Butler and Shaw 1996; Hill et al. 1996; James and Prout 1990; Morrow and Richards 1996), but a commitment to conducting research *with* children, rather than on them, necessitates further consideration of the many theoretical, methodological and ethical issues which arise. Consideration needs to be given, for example, to whether existing research methodologies and ethical positions, largely designed for adults, are appropriate when the research participant is a child (Sinclair 1996; Scott, Chapter 5) and to the fact that some issues present themselves differently, or more sharply when the participants are children. In part the difference is due to children's understanding and experience of the world being different from that of adults, and in part to the ways in which they communicate (Thomas and O'Kane 1999a). However, ultimately, the biggest challenge for researchers working with children are the disparities in power and status between adults and children (Morrow and Richards 1996). Working within a historical and cultural context in which children's voices have been marginalized, researchers face great challenges in finding ways to break down the power imbalance between adults and children, and in creating space which enables children to speak up and be heard (see Mayall, Chapter 6, and Roberts, Chapter 11).

This chapter focuses on the use of participatory techniques as one approach which can enable children and young people to talk about the sorts of issues that affect them. With a commitment to gaining a clearer understanding of the perceptions and cultural constructions of young people, the use of participatory techniques falls within the interpretive tradition of research (Bulmer, 1984) and, as this chapter explores, can enable an exploration of the similarities, as well as the differences among children's experiences in a particular social-cultural context (see Christensen and James, Chapter 8). The chapter is based on the experience of using participatory techniques with children in the middle age group (8–12 years) in a study exploring children's participation in decision-making when 'looked after' by local authorities in England and Wales and, through drawing upon the experience of researchers using participatory techniques in other cultural and social contexts, it indicates how these methods can be adapted in a variety of situations to enable greater exploration of the cultural contexts which structure children's lives.

The Context: Participatory Approaches

A variety of terms are used to describe the range of participatory approaches, from which specific tools and techniques have been adapted (see Pretty et al. 1995; Steiner 1993). However, within the context of rural development work in which such approaches have been widely used, the term 'Participatory Rural Appraisal' (PRA) has become common and while PRA may be seen as a set of techniques, it has been more widely identified as a methodology or philosophy. In contrast to the contemporary research community which operates within a prevailing positivist paradigm, PRA falls within a 'post-positivist' or 'constructivist' paradigm. Whereas conventional positivist inquiry is linear and closed, seeking to measure, aggregate and model behaviour, constructivist methodologies have been promoted for their qualitative exploratory power in providing 'depth, richness and realism of information and analysis' (Chambers 1994: 14). Rather than looking only for statistically significant relationships, one key principle of PRA is that it seeks diversity (Holland and Blackburn 1998).

Although the roots of participatory methods and approaches can be traced to many sources and traditions, five have been identified as particularly influential. These include active participatory research inspired by Paulo Freire (1972); agro-system analysis (see Conway 1987); applied anthropology; field research on farming systems; and rapid rural appraisal (see Pretty et al. 1995; Cornwall et al. 1993; and Chambers 1992). Correspondingly, PRA approaches have been used in a variety of ways. However a number of common principles underlie their use: support of local innovation, respect for diversity and complexity, enhancement of local capabilities, interactive analysis and dialogue, and support for further action (see Pretty et al. 1995). Furthermore, both researchers and researched are recognized as active participants in the collection of data, necessitating an acknowledgement of the issues of power, control and authority in the research process.

However, in seeking to involve participants in the research project 'participation does not simply imply the mechanical application of a 'technique' or method, but is instead part of a process of dialogue, action, analysis and change' (Pretty et al. 1995: 54). The successful use of participatory techniques lies in the process, rather than simply the techniques used. Thus, the genuine use of participatory techniques requires a commitment to ongoing processes of information-sharing, dialogue, reflection and action (see Theis 1996).

Up to now, participatory techniques have been most widely used in an overseas context with adults. They are particularly advantageous in communities where there are low levels of literacy, as the methods of information collection do not rely heavily on reading or writing skills, but place greater emphasis on the power of visual impressions and the active representation of ideas.

The Children and Decision-Making Study

In the particular context of this study participatory techniques were selected for their power of communication, as well as for their suitability for the project. The Children and Decision-Making Study consisted of three stages, which aimed to explore how children in their middle years who are 'looked after' by local authorities are enabled to participate in decisions about their care. The first stage involved a survey of 225 children aged 8–12 who were looked after by seven local authorities. Information was gathered from social workers to supply data about children's participation in the most recent decision-making meeting. The second stage involved a detailed study of 45 children using interviews, group discussions and participatory activities to learn more about their perspectives on decision-making processes, together with interviews with adults, and observation of meetings. The third stage *was* and still *is* concerned with the development of guidance and training resources to facilitate the inclusion of children in decision-making processes.[1]

Participatory techniques were selected as an alternative to ethnographic methods, as they were thought to be less invasive and more transparent, particularly important considerations for this project (but see Corsaro and Molinari, Chapter 9, and Davis, Watson and Cunningham-Burley, Chapter 10). First, in comparison with ethnography, where the relationship between the researcher and the researched is less defined or bound, the use of

PRA requires a more formal relationship to be established through participation in defined activities. Second, whereas the role of ethnographic researchers may change over time or be unclear, in PRA their role is transparent: the researcher is seen as the facilitator of activities (Robinson-Pat 1996). Third, rather than involving children in extensive periods of participant observation, the decision to use participatory techniques in individual and group settings meant that children (with their informed consent and permission from their carers) could dedicate specific times for their participation in the research process. Finally, in agreement with Kefyalew (1996), participatory research methods were considered innovative, fun and suitable for the study of children for, through their participation, children would be enabled to take an active role and to talk about their needs. Within the research meetings we aimed to allow the child participants a degree of control over the agenda, giving them the time and space to talk about the sorts of decisions that most affected them.

An exploration of our own perceptions of childhood, and of the differences between child and adult participants, provides further explanation as to why participatory techniques were selected as an appropriate research methodology for our goal (see James 1995; Morrow and Richards 1996; Solberg 1996). In her four-fold typology James (1995) illustrates how the way we 'see' children informs the selection of methods and techniques. She describes four models: the developing child, the tribal child, the adult child and the social child. The 'developing child' is seen as incomplete, lacking in status and relatively incompetent whereas the 'tribal child' is viewed as competent, part of an independent culture which can be studied in its own right, but not as belonging to the same communicative world as the researcher. Thus, in both these constructions children are unable to have the same status as adults. In contrast the 'adult child' and 'social child 'do have this capacity but whereas the 'adult child' is seen as socially competent in ways comparable to an adult (e.g. Alderson 1993; Bluebond-Langner 1978), the 'social child' is seen as having different, though not necessarily inferior social competencies (e.g. Johnson et al. 1995). It was with particular adherence to the 'social child' that we approached children in our study.

While stressing the uniqueness of children, the 'social child' seeks to encapsulate different domains of childhood which, as James (1995) suggests, enables us to develop research techniques which engage more effectively with children, allowing them to participate on their own terms and thereby enabling us to learn more about their experiences of the world. It has been found, for example, that children, particularly younger children, communicate well through mediums other than the verbal (e.g. James 1995; Alderson 1995) and thus it makes sense to utilize alternative forms of communication – play, activities, songs, drawing and stories. As James (1995) notes, we should make use of these different abilities rather than asking children to participate unpracticed in interviews or unasked in surveilling gaze. Talking with children about the meanings they themselves attribute to their paintings or asking them to write a story . . . allows children to engage more productively with our research questions using the talents which they, as children, possess.

(James 1995: 15)

In recognizing both the biological and structural conditions which structure children's lives, we need to develop communication strategies which engage children, build upon their own abilities and capabilities, and allow their agenda to take precedence. The use of participatory activities does precisely this.

Other research illustrates well different ways in which to establish effective communication with children: by allowing children and young people to shape the agenda; by focusing upon real life concrete events; and by involving children in 'handling things' rather than 'just talking' (Steiner 1993). Methods that have worked well have included: drawings, mapping, flow diagrams, play, matrices, transect, drama, stories and songs (Johnson 1996; James 1995; Nieuwenhuys 1996; Chawla and Kjorholt 1996; Alderson 1995; Sapkota and Sharma 1996). For example, in an action research project with street children, Nieuwenhuys (1996: 54–5) found that the 'preferred activities of children such as games, story telling and drawing may be more effective in bringing out the complexities of their experience than methods and techniques used by/with adults'. Additionally, in an ActionAid research project in Nepal, drawings allowed children 'the freedom to express views, imagination, and interpretation of the surrounding world in their own terms. Moreover the adult–child power imbalance was relatively reduced by giving full control to the child; this in turn enhanced their confidence' (Sapkota and Sharma, 1996: 61).

The use of PRA techniques are thus particularly conducive to research with children. They can assist in transforming the power relations between adults and children, enabling children to set the agenda and describe their own reality, rather than being limited by answering questions from the researcher's agenda, or trying to give 'correct' or 'best' answers. With an emphasis on the visual representation of ideas they can be designed to work with children of different ages with varied literacy skills. In thus moving away from developmental theories, which have constrained the methods of many researchers (Shaw 1996), the use of participatory techniques allows age as a construct of children's ability to participate to be minimized (Solberg 1996).

However, while participatory techniques were selected as an alternative to ethnographic methods for this study, they built upon and were used within the context of individual interviews and focus group discussions. Indeed, for

I: No.

g10: Coz I think if I sing a song it will help and if you show N [*other researcher*] the tape he might like my singing or something, coz singing does come in handy sometimes don't it?

Other children who participated in the study compared the use of participatory techniques favourably to other methods of communication used by their social workers. It became clear that many children in the middle age-group preferred methods of active communication (doing or moving), rather than passive communication ('just talking'). For example, in discussing the preparation for his review meeting during the pots and beans exercise, the following conversation took place between the interviewer and a 10-year-old boy:

I: So preparation – how many beans?
b10: This is about the meeting isn't it?
I: Yes, that's right.
b10: I'll have two.
I: So what would make it better? What would people have to do to get a three for preparation?
b10: If they bring us something for us to do – like this. So that'll be three out of three.
I: So that would really help – if you could do something like this instead of talking?
b10: Yeah.
I: . . . Have you ever been asked to fill in consultation forms?
b10: Yeah.
I: . . . Was that good – did that help?
b10: . . . Not as good as this one . . . This is the best one I've had.

In our study we also found that the use of participatory techniques facilitated explanations about the purposes of the research and the form that it will take. The activities provided a degree of transparency which displaced the 'mysticism' about research and lessened children's fears about what might happen next. Transparency is critically important in attempting to conduct good practice in research with children, just as it is one way to tackle the problematic area of 'expectations' with regards to participatory work with children. As Chawla and Kjorholt (1996: 45) observe, 'participation may indeed be an empowering process, but the limits of this power need to be acknowledged in order to make the potential for real achievements clear'. Finally, while such transparency facilitated a genuine participation by children in the research process, it also enhanced working relationships and established trust in the researchers from the children's adult caretakers. In seeking to involve children in any participatory activity it is important to gain active support from children's adult caretakers for it is through this that the child or young person may be given more space and autonomy to make choices about when and how they participate in the research.

Being given the space to take part on their own terms, many children became greatly involved in the meetings, expressing a sense of ownership of their materials and ideas, while also becoming motivated to take part in further aspects of the research process, as the extract below illustrates:

g10: Are you going to keep this grid? Can I keep this grid? Would it be OK if I took it to school tomorrow to show Miss? Because I told her you were coming and I said I would tell her what happened.

I: Yeah, I have numbered these, so if you want to set it up again to show your teacher you can do.

g10: Thanks, that would be nice.

I: If you keep it now. Then what would be useful, is if next time I come I could make a copy of it to show Nigel who I work with.

g10: Yeah, because I told Miss D [teacher] you were coming and I said if we do anything I'll ask if I could show her.

In another example, in the first interview conducted with an 8-year-old girl she decided that she wanted to keep a lot of the completed activity sheets and pocket chart. However, midway through the second interview she said:

g8: You know these sheets I kept from last time, when you said if you wanted you could take them and photocopy them – this week you can take them.

I: All right. I'll take them and photocopy them and then send them back to you. Thank you it will be nice to see them again.

A further advantage of PRA techniques is that they can aid sensitive interviewing with children. In approaching children as social actors in their own right they give them more control over what they want to talk about. For example, one 10-year-old girl commented on her preference for the building of her decision-making chart which allowed her to set the agenda, compared to other games that social workers had used which had enforced an agenda:

g10: I'm happy to talk to you another time, because it is easier to talk to someone like you than it is to talk to social workers and that about problems.

I: So why is that then?

g10: Well, mostly because they are talking about choices in my life. And this chart – they don't do stuff like that. It is harder too, because they talk to someone else – normally they talk to our mother to see if they're getting on with it. They sometimes talk to the child, but it is much harder for me to talk to the social worker.

I: . . . So what things would make it easier to talk directly to the social worker?

g10: It would make it easier if they would ask me a question and let me decide. I would make my own decision in my head – like we do on that chart. Then I could tell it to everyone I wanted to hear . . .

I: So does the chart help to talk about things?

g10: Yeah – like I decided the question and I decided what people. Because the other games they are just set questions . . . If there is a card and you pick a card – coz when you roll the dice you've got to do it. Once a card said 'have you left anyone?' That would make people upset – especially if they are fostered. So when you decide your own questions it is easier to consider, because then you won't get upset and start crying.

Participatory techniques do, however, also have their limitations. In choosing to use research techniques which are more responsive to the participants, rather than the researcher's agenda, the opportunity to gather information in a uniform way is forfeited. Though the framework of an activity can be carefully designed to ensure that a broad area of interest will be discussed, participants are given more control over the focus and agenda. In being thus responsive to individual children, the field of investigation may become limited to issues that they find significant, and/or are willing to discuss and often the reasons why certain topics are excluded may be unknown; it may be that this topic has little significance, or it may be the topic is too sensitive to talk about. Furthermore, while the use of participatory techniques may be less time-consuming than ethnographic methods, a lot of time is nonetheless required to give researchers the space to develop, use and analyse participatory techniques with children, individually and in groups. Processes of contacting, information-giving, negotiating, arrangement-making, travelling to and from, conducting interviews, analysis and feedback all require a large amount of time and resources.

With regards to the suitability of using participatory techniques with children of different ages and abilities, as we have shown, a range of participatory techniques can be adapted to suit children and young people of varying ages, with a variety of literacy, oracy or conceptual skills. However, some techniques clearly still require a certain level of conceptual or physical ability (see Davis, Watson and Cunningham-Burley, Chapter 10). For example, in our study two children with some learning difficulties were able to make their own decision-making chart, particularly when given more time. Yet, the researchers were less able to engage another two children who had more severe learning difficulties in this activity, as its conceptual nature proved too difficult. However, the use of pictures rather than words in all of the activities may assist in their appropriateness when literacy skills are an issue (see Christensen and James, Chapter 8).

In both the 'movement evaluations' and evaluation forms children expressed the importance of 'fun' as a factor which describes how interesting a research meeting is.[5] For example, the range of feedback from 'your thoughts about the day' evaluation forms from ten young people attending one activity day included the following descriptions:

> fun (×7); enjoyable (×5); funny (×4); exciting (×4); cool (×4); good (×2); excellent (×2); ace (×2); amazing (×2); fantastic (×2); terrific (×2); great(×2); made new friends (×2); a laugh; smart; not how I expected – I thought it would be just talking; it was more activity than just talking; not bad; tiring; I liked the good communication; it was in blocks – not one load; discuss a lot; helped; educational; brilliant; playful; the games were good; fantasy; Claire is good; Nigel is funny; I liked it.

However, with the 'fun' element there is also the danger that participatory techniques may be taken less seriously. Participatory techniques should not be labelled as 'childish' techniques but seen, rather, as child-centred.

Conclusion

Article 12 of the United Nations Convention on the Rights of the Child 1989 clearly states that children and young people have a right to be involved in decisions which affect them. This right extends from decisions affecting them as individuals, to decisions which affect them as a collectivity – an acknowledgement that they are social actors in their own lives. Social researchers can play an important role in embracing this challenge to create space for children and young people to be listened to and heard and, as this chapter has advocated, the use of participatory techniques can facilitate such a task. If 'understanding children and childhood, . . . requires listening attentively to their agendas, and participating with them in the research process' then participatory techniques provide one frame-work which is responsive, has open-ended research goals and allows children to set their own agenda (Hood et al. 1996: 118). Furthermore, these methods can be adapted to suit work across a wide age range of children and young people, and can be used in a wide range of settings.

Information gathered with children through the use of participatory techniques in our study has drawn attention to a wide range of matters which concern children while also highlighting a range of contemporary theoretical issues concerning the nature of childhood and adult-child relations (see Thomas and O'Kane 1999b). Thus while reinforcing messages

methodological triangulation through allowing the researcher to assess the extent to which a group of children share a particular attitude or opinion which has been randomly gleaned by the researcher from a casual comment made in passing or overheard.

The graphic tools which we developed can, we suggest, be added to this range of visual research methods and indeed extend the potential for research with children. What the 'tools' did was to enable children to participate in the research process by creating images for themselves, which were about themselves. This confirms that one of the most important features of these 'tools' is that they work to mediate the communication between the researcher and the children. First and very practically, as noted, the tools permitted the concretizing of the very abstract notions of time use. Second, the tools provided another medium of communication over and above that of talking. Rather than employing the more adult-centred frame of the interview or conversation, we utilized one unified form – the circle – and drew upon children's own competences and skills with pens and paper to express their experiences of being 10 years old; of being a pupil at school'; of living in families; and of residing in a village or an urban neighbourhood. As we shall go on to show, it is out of this commonality of method that the diversities which exist between them was first revealed. Third, using the tools gave children the opportunity to offer a commentary on, not only the final image on the page as they might do about a photograph or a picture, but also the process of producing it. These visual tools provide, therefore, a rich, multilayered and mediated form of communication which is facilitated both by the image and by its very process of production.

It is the form and process of using the tools that we consider in the next section, taking account of the theoretical proposition offered by Rapport that

> individual contents and cultural forms constitute one social reality that cannot be properly or ideally described in the absence of the other . . . it is their meeting in opposition which is socially constitutive.
>
> (Rapport 1993: 164–5)

He suggests that culture can be described as a 'fund of behavioural forms' within which, nonetheless, can be seen 'complex and often diverse individual world-views' (Rapport 1993: 165). Here we show how the children drew on two particular communal forms of representation to complete the 'My Week' task. One of these derives from their common experiences and competences of everyday school practice. The other has its basis in children's own cultural practices of drawing, doodling and copying. It is the commonality of these forms which, we suggest, enabled the children to offer to us their own subjective account of time use in their everyday life.

My Week: Being a Schooled Child

The 'My Week' tool was particularly revealing about the commonality which children share as 'school children'. More directly, it recalled in them a shared and common educational history. Most of the children immediately likened the circle to the familiar mathematical concept of a 'pie chart' which they had encountered in maths and geography lessons at school. As one boy confidently said when he was presented with the piece of paper: '[I've] done that before.' In this sense, then, this particular drawing activity highlighted a similarity of experience among the 10-year-old children: that of solving a problem through working with a pie chart.

However, in that this skill – doing a pie chart – had been developed in the context of schooling, it was one which, unlike more general drawing, carried with it aspects of the 'hidden curriculum' of the schooling process, a factor which, in turn, shaped the way in which the children carried out the task. For some children the task was viewed as being akin to a school task and thus suspiciously subject to the regulatory devices and regimes which control the production of work for children within school. When seen in this way, what was a shared and common experience threatened, from the children's point of view, to become one which potentially marked out their difference in skill from one another. Thus, negotiating their way around this potential point of divisiveness also became part of the process of completing 'My Week' and revealed, to the researchers, the diversities in terms of educational competences which arise for children through the daily, shared experience of schooling.

Some children, boys in particular, were very exacting in the execution of 'My Week', treating it as a geometrical exercise or a mathematical task: they used rulers to draw straight lines, asked for rubbers to remove the trace of lines drawn in error and checked with the researcher that they were doing it right. Despite every effort being made to reassure the children that there was not in fact a correct way in which to complete the task, many children nonetheless carried it out according to such an agenda. They continued to seek guidance, asking 'Can you . . . ?', 'Do you just . . . ?' as they set about completing the task. One girl asked, 'Shall I just put school?', enquiring whether that large period of time identified as 'school time' needed to be subdivided into its different phases of 'play time' and 'work time'.

Such questioning and checking for reassurance, however, does not suggest that children were incompetent in carrying out the task – all the children were able to successfully complete it. Rather, such questioning draws upon the hierarchical relations that already exist between adults and children, and in particular between teachers and pupils at school. These position children as having only a relative competence and one which, moreover, is subject to teachers' continual judgement and assessment.

But the framing of the task by the children's communal experiences of the school curriculum and of being a 'schooled' and disciplined child is perhaps most clearly seen in the following question often asked by the children towards the end of the task: 'Do you put your name on it?' It is through the naming of their work that children both claim their authorship of it at school and are made responsible for it. The naming of a piece of work permits the progress of an individual child to be assessed; as each piece of work is submitted to the teacher the log of marks, checked off against names, records the child's progress through the school year. Through this process are mapped the diversities in intellectual and academic achievement that exist between children.

My Week: Being a Competent Child

The shared discourse of schooling described above, which framed the completion of the 'My Week' task for some children, had the potential to reveal differences between them with regard to their competence as school children. However, the task also made use of children's shared skills as children. This can be seen through the different ways in which the charts were created which represented almost an antidote to school work, through drawing on less legitimized practices of schooling – free drawing, doodling and copying.

It is significant, we suggest, that many of the children chose to complete 'My Week' using drawings rather than words. Drawing or doodling was seen by the children in the schools where the study was carried out as an ordinary, rather than specialized, activity – as something which they just do, as something with which children routinely fill up time on their own or in the company of others. Being able to draw does not necessarily mean having a particular skill in using a representational device. Neither does it always represent a mark of personal artistic achievement. As they draw children happily chat with one another and in this sense drawing can be an accompaniment to socializing. As cultural practice among children, unlike among adults, it is something which children expect to be able to do and also enjoy doing and it was clear that the children themselves considered 'all' children to be competent at it.

This understanding was rather poignantly brought home to one of the researchers during one wet playtime when the children had to stay in the classroom out of the rain. Being a time in the day marked out as non-lesson time, children were permitted to read comics or do other recreational activities. Common among these was to draw. A group of children engaged the researcher's attention as she sat with them at the table:

C: Would you like to do some drawing?
R: Yes.
C: [*busily drawing*] What are you going to draw?

The researcher, pencil in hand, was suddenly nonplussed. She realized, rather belatedly, that she did not know 'how' to draw in the way that the children did. It was a skill which she no longer had. Trained in art, for her as for many adults, drawing had come to involve an act of interpretation, usually from material object to visual representation on a page rather than a 'free flowing' experiential activity.

Thus, although some children are, of course, recognized by their peers to be exceptionally 'good at drawing', drawing is generally regarded by them as a non-specialist skill. This means that a child's drawing, unlike their spelling or neat hand writing is less open to be critiqued or judged by others, including other children. Drawing falls outside the educational framework of presentational skills, of 'success' and 'failure', of 'right' or 'wrong', the framework through which academic achievement is commonly experienced by children. In this sense then the insertion by children of pictures in the pie charts could be seen as a strategy to mask the different competences revealed in their writing (Figure 8.2).

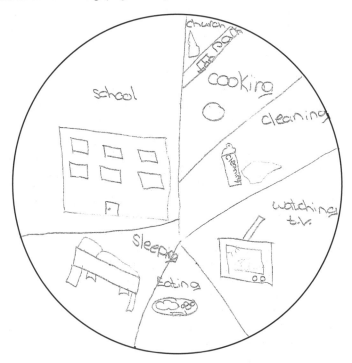

Figure 8.2 'My Week': girl aged 10

Other potential differences between children were elided in another way. Some children, for example, chose to work in pairs, deciding together what should be included on the charts and how information should be displayed. Although such a collaborative effort clearly detracts therefore from the usefulness of the data as representing an account of each particular child's week, these ways of using the tool tell us something further about children's own views concerning difference and similarity, diversity and uniformity. As noted elsewhere (James 1993; Christensen 1999) a sense of sameness is important for children, providing for them a feeling of belonging, a way in which to smooth over the potential which any personal diversity or deviation might have to rupture the social relations which exist between one child and another. 'Copying' each other thus masks any potential differences among children, inducing a sense of sharing both in the process of making the chart and in the presentation of the final product. Whereas children 'working together' is encouraged as a skill that children need to develop more generally within the class room it is a working practice that is nonetheless discouraged, and indeed disapproved of, in those lessons when tasks are meant to be completed by children independently (Christensen 1999).

That the children chose to copy each other when doing the 'My Week' in the context of the school room – a space where such a practice is not usually permitted – may, in itself, register yet other aspects of childhood's diversities and similarities. It may, for example, reveal how the children are differentiating between the various temporal frameworks at work within the school, that which governs lessons and that in which the more recreational tasks are located. In this sense, participating in the research was perhaps defined by the children as 'not working'. In this time space, they judged 'copying' to be permitted. It received no sanction from the researcher as, indeed, neither did a refusal to do the task! In this sense, then, children's production of similarity by copying can be seen as children choosing to treat the space and time framed by the researcher as children's own time, allowing them to do things in the way they wished to. This was in opposition to the 'curriculum time' of the school day, where they would have to do what was required of them (Christensen et al. 1999). Thus, although clearly for some children the discursive practices of the educational setting of 'My Week' framed the way they completed it, leading as we have shown to the revelation of shared experiences between them, for most children completing the task became something through which they expressed their idiosyncrasies, personal skills and their varied social experiences (Figure 8.3).

For example, perhaps affirming Walkerdine's (1985) observation that the structuring of girls' identities at school is largely as 'good girls', in contrast to the boisterous boys' identities as 'real boys', it was often the girls who asked for most reassurance from the researchers. One girl checked continually on her progress as she completed the task:

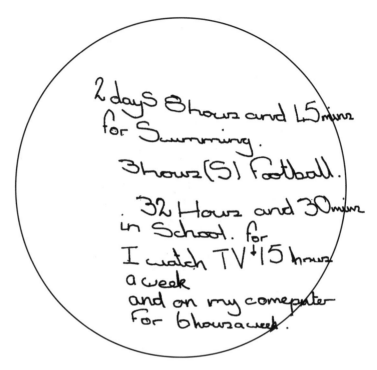

Figure 8.3 'My Week': boy aged 10 (a competitive swimmer)

Shall I just leave it like that?

Shall I do it in pen?

Can you put 'school'?

And, the final reassurance:

Is it a double M in swimming?

Most boys, on the other hand, seemed less concerned with whether they were doing it right. Having decided it was a pie chart, they carried out the task with confidence. Their concern was directed at the product, the final image which they produced. Thus, many of the boys were keen to devise the chart with a scientific accuracy, to the extent in some cases of using a pro-tractor to ensure that each segment was as an exact account of time spent as possible (Figure 8.4):

B: Er . . . that's about right for eating, all of these are right 'cos I divided [it] up into twenty-four things and then.

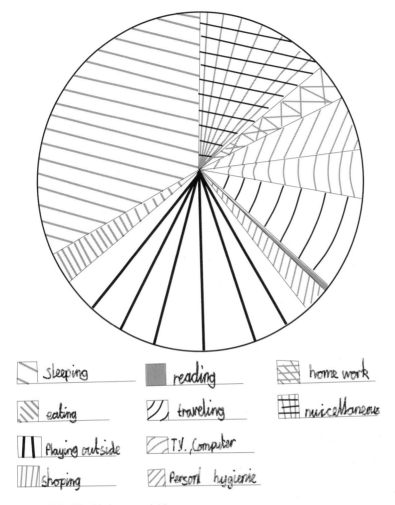

⬚ sleeping	⬛ reading	⬚ home work
⬚ eating	⬚ traveling	⬚ miscellaneous
⬚ Playing outside	⬚ T.V. Computer	
⬚ shoping	⬚ Personl hygienie	

Figure 8.4 'My Week': boy aged 10

R: Twenty-four hours?
B: And then, er, I say, so that's nine hours sleeping and then, er six, no eight hours outside and then like the other things.

However, it is clear that other diversities, beyond those of gender, were revealed in the process of children putting pencil to paper. Although most children quickly took charge over and responsibility for structuring the task, they would continually keep an eye on how other children in the group undertook the task. This they did through a process of comparing their work with another's and remarking on the differences and similarities

171

they could observe between them. For example, one boy looking at his neighbour's chart, enquired: 'Why are you colouring it in?' His own circle was simply left black and white, thus differing from the multicoloured diagram of his neighbour. Another boy decided to make a key for his chart with which to unlock its content: 'I'm doing a key!', he announced proudly. In these ways the uniform task of making a pie chart revealed an array of diverse forms, expressive of children's individuality as children, of their personal and social experiences of an ordinary week. Sometimes, as we show in the next section, through this process the children themselves became aware that they had different experiences of being 10 years old.

Children as Reflexive Interpreters

While introducing a science lesson a teacher involved in our research observed to the children: 'Every graph has a story to tell. It is not just a pretty pattern.' In this way, she wished to alert the children to the deeper layer of information that a graph represents. But she also wished to signal its difference from 'pictures' produced while doodling or drawing. This observation is pertinent to our understanding of the 'My Week' charts, which the children produced: while many were, indeed, pretty patterns they all also had stories to tell. However, the teacher's dismissal of the aesthetic in favour of the rational account is unwarranted for, as we shall detail below, some of the charts not only spoke eloquently about the particularities of individual children's lives, but also helped to detail the experiences which children have in common with one another and those that make up childhood's diversity. Thus, we suggest that attention has to be paid to data as a compilation of content, form and the research process through which they have been produced. As we discuss below, an important part of this process was the children's reflexive critique about their own progressive understanding of the task they were completing. For example, while filling in her 'My Week' chart one girl kept up a continuous monitoring of her own progress: 'My pen's running out. I have to fit Monday all in there, Oh my god, Monday, Tuesday, Wednesday, Thursday, Friday. I can put Monday in there'. A boy, half way through, critically assessed his own chart, saying: 'I did that wrong'. He then redrew the segments so that the chart more accurately expressed that which he wished to say. Another boy justified his chart in the following way: 'That's divided into six 'cos we have six hours in school.' He then carefully divided the segment into units representing the different days of the week and wrote in each space what he did at school each day.

These observations underscore the importance of seeing children as competent interpretive social actors when participating in research (see Corsaro and Molinari, Chapter 9), a point which can be exemplified further through an analysis of the content of the charts which reveal children's conceptions of time and their social experience of time use.

For example, most of the children did not put divisions such as 'sleep time' or 'meal time' on their charts. Indeed, for many, the representation of 'sleeping' seemed particularly problematic, for the children had already experienced 'sleeping' as a 'time' when one is not conscious of 'time' at all! As one boy observed: 'It feels like you're, just like that: you're going to sleep and you just woke up.' However, some of the children were, nonetheless, keen to explore this aspect of time use. One boy showed the researcher his chart as he was filling it in:

B: That [amount of] time in bed?
R: Um, it probably is that much time actually . . .
B: I've put the bed on that side?
R: Yes, you can do.
B: So if I go to bed at about, say about nine erm . . .
R: You don't have to make it very, very accurate.
B: . . . forty-eight hours.

A similar concern to explore in detail the quantities of time which particular kinds of activities take up was demonstrated by other children too and reveals the power of graphic techniques to permit the expression of children's growth in awareness of their time use:

R: So, how did you find out whether this was sort of about two hours maybe eating a week, no a day isn't it?
B: No, that would be about an hour!
R: An hour, OK.
B: Like, twenty minutes.
R: For each meal?
B: Yeah.
R: So, you sort of sat and thought, 'Well, how much time do I use?'
B: Yeah.
R: You didn't use a watch to time yourself?
B: No . . . I sort of guessed.

Besides 'sleeping' and 'eating', most of the charts also did not include everyday routine activities such as washing oneself, going to the toilet, brushing one's hair, and so on. These did, however, appear on one boy's chart but, significantly, he had taken his chart home and engaged his mother as a co-respondent:

R: Tim, how did you make yours, how was your mum involved in doing it?

T: Erm, she like figured out the percentages with me and she gave me the idea for that, she gave me some of the idea, for most of these, like personal hygiene.

However, that such everyday activities are excluded from most children's charts is highly suggestive: it indicates that children's own awareness of time use was indeed prompted by the 'My Week' chart. Until his mother intervened it had not occurred to Tim that coping with 'personal hygiene' actually took up a particular amount of time in the week (Figure 8.4). Second, noting what the children omitted from their charts provides more general insight into the cultural meaning of time for children. Two boys were comparing their charts:

Joe: Well, I know sleeping was correct 'cos I figured it out on a calculator, and reading's right and so's travelling but all these lot are random but they're about right I reckon.

Michael decides to challenge his chart:

Michael: I think reading's wrong, I think that's wrong.

Joe retaliates, insisting that it is his view that is being asked for and that, in his opinion, his own assessment of the time he spent reading is correct:

Michael: Reading, yeah that's your opinion and playing outside.

However, the question which Michael then retreats with reveals both the reason for his initial challenge of Joe's estimation and, at the same time, illustrates that children may attach particular values to certain forms of time use. In effect, Michael is attempting to seek out an explanation, through his challenge, for why 'reading' featured such a lot on Joe's chart.

Michael: Did you spend a lot of time on your own over half term or . . . ?

It is clear from Michael's incredulous query that, in his view, only someone who *had* to pass a lot of time alone could possibly have such a large segment set aside for reading. However, Joe quickly denied this:

Joe: Um, no not really. I was mainly outside most of the time and at my friend's house and everything.

In his reply Joe defended the accuracy of his chart while nonetheless confirming the importance for children of presenting themselves as sociable, as someone with friends, rather than as someone who sits inside on his own reading.

Two final examples relate to children's experience of time as 'flow' punctuated by 'happenings' which, we suggest, largely emanate from children's contact with the institutional structures through which childhood is framed. A conversation between the researcher and Maria is revealing in this respect:

Maria: Can you put things that [*pauses*] I like to do when you sometimes . . .

Unfortunately, Maria was at this point interrupted by the researcher who, at first, thought Maria meant: Can you put things down when you only do them sometimes? Later the conversation revealed, however, that drawing – the activity in question – was one that Maria liked to do 'all the time'. It was in this sense a habitual weekly activity which she spent much time doing. This misunderstanding is revealing. Seen in this new light Maria's question makes a quite subtle distinction between those things that she did regularly during the week – activities which emanate from social and institutional structures such as going to school, playing rugby, doing housework – and those regular activities that were less structured and not imposed upon her. These were the things she enjoyed doing and chose to do herself. In this sense then the distinction made by Maria was between activities so closely related to the experiential 'flow' of everyday time that only with difficulty could they be located within an exact time frame and those 'happenings' which are significantly bound to a temporal and spatial structure. Drawing represents for Maria an activity which she is likely to drift in and out of in between having to do other things; it is one which she is not obliged to do, but one she has some own control over.

Similarly revelatory moments occurred with respect to the experience of being 10 years old. Although sharing numerical age the very differences in respect to children's competence and maturity which 'My Week' revealed made two girls reflect on the ample differences of social experience between them. (The girls knew each other well from their shared everyday life at school.) After thinking for a short while about what her week consisted of one of the girls turned to the researcher and said: 'I've only put four things down!' The researcher explored with the girl whether she had indeed left out some things which she might want to add to her chart by asking the girl more exacting questions such as: 'Do you do any cooking at home?' This prompted the girl to reflect further on her weekly activities and yielded a much longer list which showed that she was expected to make a large contribution to household work: on a regular basis she looked after the cat and dog, laid the table, washed the pots, cleaned her bedroom, made her bed and often did some cooking. Her friend, working next to her, and listening in on the conversation then revealed that she only had to look after her cat and rabbit, that her mum made her bed for her and that cooking was something she only occasionally helped with. In this way the two girls were suddenly made aware of their very different home lives and the contributions that were expected of them. In such concretization lies, then, the potential for increasing children's own awareness about the shared and the diverse aspects of children's social experiences which such 'tools' may facilitate.

Conclusion

This chapter has argued that although children may share in a common biology and follow a broadly similar developmental path, their social experiences and their relative competences as social actors must always be seen as contextualized, rather than determined, by the process of physiological and psychological change. Through exploring the use of a specific research technique we have exemplified the scope for achieving a better understanding of the diversities as well as commonalities of childhood and the importance of acknowledging the interrelationship between the form, content and process of research.

Thus, as we showed, providing a uniform and specific model – a blank circle – allowed children to work as individuals within the relative fixity of its conceptual form. Children designed visual images of their weekly time within two shared frames of reference – that of schooling and that of children's own practices and peer relations – and in this way drew on common social skills and competences to represent their own individual and everyday social experiences. This process, as we have also demonstrated, showed children as actively interpreting and reflecting on the research they take part in and thereby potentially gaining new insight into their own and other children's social experiences and practices.

In thus showing how commonality and diversity intersect we have seriously called into question the use of 'age' as a dominant signifier when accounting for and understanding the shape and experience of children's everyday lives. In this sense, then, the methodology of this piece of research will allow us to contribute to the debate about the sensitivity of global developmental paradigms in accounting for children's own experiences and the local conditions of childhood. Global paradigms, it is suggested, may over-standardize models of childhood as a particular segment of the life course by according priority to age and thus induce a determined and determining conformity which might underplay the impact of local social and environmental contexts on the everyday lives and experiences of children. The consequences of such global models may be, then, to privilege commonality above diversity, with such a privileging turning out to be potentially detrimental and socially excluding of some children.

Acknowledgements

This chapter draws on findings from 'Changing Times', a research project, which the two authors are currently undertaking with Chris Jenks,

Goldsmiths College, London. The study is funded under the ESRC research programme Children 5–16: Growing into the 21st Century.

Notes

1 The tools were used alongside interviews and participant observation, which took place in primary and secondary schools in a rural and an urban area of Northern England. The twelve month fieldwork period covered the time of transition from primary to secondary school when, it was thought, children's experiences, use and organization of time would change considerably. Towards the end of the project a large-scale quantitative survey was conducted in both these settings, drawing on the key findings of the qualitative study.
2 The choice of a circle to represent a week clearly has embedded with it notions of cyclical, repetitive time. However, though we acknowledge that such a representation therefore has the potential to shape children's thinking, it was apparent to us that by the age of 10 children were already familiar with different cultural notions of time – for example, that time has a value and should not be wasted; that the life course can be figuratively represented in linear form with a unidirectional movement from birth to death. Through giving children the circle as a prompt to their thinking about time we drew upon this cultural repertoire. However, that children also chose to disrupt or ignore the circular form suggests that it did not limit or restrict the expression of their ideas.

References

Chambers, R. (1992) *Rural Appraisal: Rapid, Relaxed and Participatory*, IDS Discussion Paper 311, Brighton: Institute of Development Studies.

Chambers, R. (1994) *Participatory Rural Appraisal: Challenges, Potentials and Paradigms*, Brighton: Institute of Development Studies.

Christensen, P. (1998) 'Difference and similarity: how children's competence is constituted in illness and its treatment', in I. Hutchby. and J. Moran-Ellis (eds) *Children and Social Competence: Arenas of Action*, London: Falmer Press.

Christensen, P. (1999) 'Towards an anthropology of childhood sickness: an ethnographic study of Danish school children', Ph.D. thesis, Hull University.

Christensen, P., James, A. and Jenks, C. (1999) ' "All we needed to do was to blow the whistle": Children's embodiment of time', in S. Cunningham-Burley (ed.) *Making Sense of the Body*, London: Macmillan.

Hallinan, M. (1981) 'Recent advances in sociometry', in S.R. Asher and J.M. Gottman (eds) *The Development of Children's Friendships*, Cambridge: Cambridge University Press.

James, A. (1993) *Childhood Identities: Self and Social Relationships in the Experience of the Child*, Edinburgh: Edinburgh University Press.

James, A., Jenks, C. and Prout, A. (1998) *Theorising Childhood*, Cambridge: Polity.

Mauthner, M. (1997) 'Methodological aspects of collecting data from children: lessons from three research projects', *Children and Society* 11(1): 16–29.

Prosser, J. (ed.) (1998) *Image-based Research*, London: Falmer Press.

Rapport, N. (1993) *Diverse World Views in an English Village*, Edinburgh: Edinburgh University Press.

Pia Christensen and Allison James

Richardson, S.A., Goodman, N., Hastorf, A.H. and Dornbusch, S.M. (1961) 'Cultural uniformities in reaction to physical disabilities', *American Sociological Review* 26: 241–6.

Walkerdine, V. (1985) 'Child development and gender; the making of teachers and learners in the classroom', in *Early Childhood Education: History, Policy and Practice*, Bulmershe Research Publication 4, Reading: Bulmershe College of Higher Education.

Wetton, N.N. and McWhirter, J. (1998) 'Images and curriculum development in health education', in J. Prosser (ed.) *Image-based Research*, London: Falmer Press.

Woodhead, M. (1999) 'Reconstructing developmental psychology', *Children and Society* 13(1): 3–19.

9 Entering and Observing in Children's Worlds:

A Reflection on a Longitudinal Ethnography of Early Education in Italy

William A. Corsaro and Luisa Molinari

Introduction

In this chapter we evaluate theoretical and methodological issues in conducting longitudinal ethnographies of young children. We do this by reflecting on and examining field entry and data collection in the initial phase of our recent study of children's transition from preschool to elementary school in Modena, Italy. The following vignette based on field notes from Bill Corsaro's earlier research in Bologna, Italy serves to introduce the goals of our discussion in this chapter.

> Several years ago I returned to a preschool in Bologna, Italy, several months after completing a year long ethnographic study of peer culture there. The anticipation of my return had been peaked by an exchange of letters with the children and teachers. Upon my arrival I was greeted by the children and teachers, who presented me with a large poster upon which they had drawn my image and printed: 'Ben Tornato, Bill!' (Welcome back, Bill!) After handing me the poster the children swarmed around me, pulled me down to my knees and each child took a turn embracing and kissing me. In the midst of the jubilation I noticed a few new faces – 3 year olds who had entered the school during my absence. One or two of these little ones shyly came up to touch me or to receive a kiss.
>
> Later in the day after the commotion had settled, I was sitting at a table with several children who were playing a board game. I noticed a small boy, who I later learned was named Alberto, eyeing me from a distance. He finally came over and asked: 'Sei Bill, veramente?' (Are you really Bill?). 'Yes, I'm really Bill,' I responded in Italian. Alberto, smiling, looked me over for a few seconds and then ran off to play with some other children.

One important aspect of the vignette for our discussion is the nature of Bill's relation to the preschool children and his participant status in the local peer and school cultures. The children's jubilant marking of Bill's return to the school was certainly related to the length of his absence – absence does indeed make the heart grow fonder. However, the closeness of Bill's relationship with the children went well beyond the joy accompanying the return of an old friend. Several ethnographers of children have pointed to the importance of developing a participant status as an atypical, less powerful adult in research with young children (Corsaro 1985, 1996; Fine and Sandstrom 1988; Mandell 1988; see also Mayall, Chapter 6, and Davis Watson and Cunnigham-Burley, Chapter 10). As we shall go on to show, in this case Bill's very 'foreignness' was central to his participant status. His limited competencies in the Italian language and his lack of knowledge of the workings of the school led the children to see him as an 'incompetent adult' who they could take under their wings to show the ropes. They also saw his initial communicative difficulties with the teachers, and discovered that they were better at educating him about things than their teachers were. Thus, the children claimed him as one of their own, telling their parents: 'We can talk to Bill and the teachers can't!' Word of this *'famoso Bill'*, as one parent referred to him, quickly spread to the children's families.

A second important aspect of the story which we draw out from this is its capturing of the importance of longitudinal ethnography for theory generation in the sociology of childhood. Recent theoretical work in this area is critical of traditional theories of socialization and child development for their marginalization of children. Traditional views focus on individual development and see the child as incomplete – as in the process of movement from immaturity to adult competence. The new approaches eschew the individualistic bias of traditional theories and stress the importance of collective action and social structure. In line with these new theoretical views, we have offered the notion of interpretive reproduction (Corsaro 1992, 1993, 1997). From this perspective we argue that the whole time children are developing individually, the collective processes that they are a part of are also changing. These processes are collectively produced by children and adults in the many interwoven local cultures making up children's lives. Sociologists need to address these collective processes developmentally or longitudinally and to document the nature of children's membership in these local cultures and their changing degrees or intensities of membership and participation over time and across social institutions. Longitudinal ethnography is an ideal method for such a theoretical approach, particularly when it aims to both document children's evolving membership in their culture (Lave and Wenger 1991) and when focused on key transition periods in children's lives. Bill's return to the school was his first attempt to extend the longitudinal design of our research toward this ideal.

Let us return to our story to consider the richness of longitudinal ethnography. Bill did not simply return to his field site and renew his research. Traces of his continued presence were sketched by the children and teachers in their reflective talk about their past experiences with him. The memories and emotions evoked by these informally occasioned discourses were deepened and intensified by a series of more focused activities: their reading and discussing of letters and cards sent by the researcher; their construction and enjoyment of a gift from him (a Halloween mobile of swaying jack-o-lanterns, witches, spiders and ghosts along with a description of the wondrous but foreign children's holiday symbolized in the mobile); their composition of letters and art work to send to Bill; their discussion and anticipation of his return; and their construction of the poster to commemorate the 'homecoming'. A version of these discourses and activities was also produced in Bill's world, in his discussions in his family, with his colleagues, with his students and in his research reports.

We argue that the homecoming did not mark the beginning of a new phase of a longitudinal study, but rather a continuing evolution of the researcher's membership in this group. In turn, the documentation of and reflection on this evolution is of central theoretical importance for grasping both cognitively and emotionally the nature of the children's evolving membership in the local peer and school cultures of this educational institution. Thus, we see the inextricable connection of theory and method in ethnographic research.

Finally, there is the ending of our story and the young boy, Alberto. In his interactions with his peers and teachers over the course of his first year, this mysterious Bill had become somewhat of a legend to Alberto. Thus, Alberto, being somewhat of a doubting Thomas, desired direct confirmation of his status. Alberto's interest in and fascination with Bill illustrate how the participant status of the ethnographer becomes embedded in the network of personal relations of those he or she studies over time in longitudinal research. Although Alberto needed to confirm the reality of Bill's existence, he was very much influenced by what he had learned about him from the other children. For example, he quickly seized on and relished in Bill's status as an incompetent adult. A few days after Bill's return several children were telling him about something that had occurred during his absence. The story had to be halted and repeated several times because Bill had trouble understanding. During the last retelling, Alberto joined the group and threw up his hands laughing: 'Ma uffa! Bill. Lui non capisce niente!' (Oh brother! Bill. He doesn't understand anything). It becomes somewhat easier to empathize with the lower status of children in society when, as an adult, one finds oneself the butt of successful teasing at the hands of a 3 year old.

The following sections of this chapter parallel the three main points of our introductory story: entering the field and developing a participant status with the children and teachers in the preschool; documenting our evolving membership in the local cultures in this setting; and identifying and participating in the priming events which prepare the children for their coming transition to elementary school.

Field Entry, Acceptance and Participant Status

Field entry is crucial in ethnography because one of its central goals as an interpretive method is the establishment of membership status and an insider's perspective (Corsaro 1996; Rizzo et al. 1992). In research in educational settings with young children these goals depend on: dealing with and developing the trust of a range of adult gatekeepers; acquiring working knowledge of the social structure, nature of interpersonal relations, and daily routines in the setting; and gaining the acceptance of the teachers and children.

Dealing with Gatekeepers

Our research in the *scuola dell'infanzia* was based on what Schatzman and Strauss (1973: 22) have called 'mutually voluntary and negotiated entrée' in that our hosts (the director, teachers and parents) held 'options not only to prevent entrée but to terminate relations with' us at almost any point thereafter. Because these adults had varying degrees of control over our access to the research site and the activities of the children, we refer to them as gatekeepers (Corsaro 1985).

The collaborative nature of our research was of clear importance in negotiations with gatekeepers. We had worked together on several earlier studies and pooled our data on observations in the Italian *asilo nido* (for 1–3 year olds: Luisa Molinari) and the *scuola dell'infanzia* (Bill Corsaro) to study the emergence and extension of peer culture among Italian preschool children (Corsaro and Molinari 1990; Molinari and Corsaro 1994). In the present study, Luisa negotiated field entry with the director of the preschool, the first grade principal, and the preschool and first grade teachers. Together we presented our research aims and described the study to parents and later presented interim reports of initial findings to the teachers, parents and interested members of the community. Luisa's knowledge of the preschool and elementary school systems in Modena (she is the mother of three young children who are at various points in these systems) was essential in developing initial rapport with the gatekeepers and in navigating through the bureaucracy of early education in Italy.

An obvious question arises here: why did not Luisa, who was native to the culture and this region of Italy, conduct the ethnographic research? Aside from the fact that Bill had a great deal more experience as an ethnographer of young children, there is another (perhaps more important) reason for our collaboration in this way. The ethnographer's acceptance into the world of children is especially difficult because of obvious differences between adults and children in terms of cognitive and communicative maturity, power and physical size. As noted earlier, however, Bill's 'adult incompetence' helped in overcoming many of these obstacles to becoming accepted and drawn into children's everyday lives in his earlier work in Bologna. In fact, we would argue that one of the strengths of cross-cultural ethnographies of children is that the foreign ethnographer is often seen as a less threatening adult by children and young people (see also Berentzen 1995; Wulf, 1988).[1]

Acceptance and Participant Status in the Peer Culture

Bill's initial days in the *scuola dell'infanzia* in Modena were a new challenge for him. For the first time he entered a preschool setting where he was the only true novice. In past research he had entered schools at the start of the term and at least some (if not all) of the children were, like him, new to the setting. Furthermore, in this instance not only was he entering the group at the midpoint of the school year, but also almost all of the children and teachers had already been together for two and a half years. This fact coupled with his 'foreignness' led many of the children and adults to be very curious about him during his first days at the school.

Bill was introduced to the children by the teachers as someone from America who was going to come to the school often until the end of the year in June. As he had done in past research Bill's main strategy of entering the children's culture was to move into play areas, sit down and let the children react to him (see Corsaro 1985). Several of the older and more active children in the group (Luciano, Elisa and Marina) often told Bill what was happening and generally took charge of him during the first few weeks. They escorted him to the music and English classes, and Bill overheard them making references to his presence to children in the other 5-year-old and the 4-year-old classes and reporting that: 'Bill would be a part of their class.'

Over the first week at the school Bill also got to know all the other children as he participated in a number of activities. For example, during his second day at the school he was seated next to a girl, Sandra, during morning snack. After they finished a snack of sliced apples, Valerio began handing out candy that he had brought as a treat to the other children. Bill was a bit disappointed that Valerio did not offer him a piece of candy, rather passing him by and handing one to Sandra and then moving on to the other children. Sandra said she did not like the kind that Valerio gave her and Bill suggested she ask him to exchange it. When Valerio had finished passing out the candy, Sandra called him over and asked for a chocolate candy and Valerio gave it to her and took back the fruit candy. Sandra smiled at Bill, clearly happy with this outcome. Bill smiled back even though he still had not received any candy.

This incident captures the complexity of field entry. Even though Bill had been trying hard to escape the usual form of adult–child relationship at the school, in this instance he was clearly put in his place as an adult. Bill's failure to be included in the sharing of the sweets was no doubt related to Valerio's perception of the uncertainty of his participant status in the routine (i.e. the sweets were usually shared only with other children). However, Bill's support of Sandra's attempt to get a particular flavour of candy did send the message that he was not a typical adult and that he was aware of subtle negotiations among peers in the routine.

Before long Bill was drawn more fully into peer activities. Later in his first week at the school he joined a group of boys who were playing with building materials. Consider the following example drawn from field notes.

Example 1
February 13, 1996

Renato, Angelo, Mario, and Dario are playing with plastic, grooved building materials. They hand me some of the materials and ask if I can get them apart. I accept this task willingly, but soon realize that the pieces are stuck together much tighter than I realized. In fact, I first push with all my might with no success. One of the teachers, Giovanna, now walks by, laughs, and says the children have found a practical use for me. I now realize that many of the pieces have probably been stuck together for a long time. Just about the time I am about ready to give up, I try holding one piece on the edge of the table with the other hanging over the edge. I push hard and the pieces pop apart. Angelo and Renato yell: 'Bravo Bill!,' and then immediately hand me several more pieces. I easily separate the first two with my inventive method, but then I run into trouble again as several pieces will just not budge. Meanwhile the boys are copying my method with some success, so I keep at it. I then notice that Angelo and Mario are gathering up all the separated pieces and are putting them back in the box. They tell several other children that Bill got them apart, but they are not to play with them. I wonder about this. Are they afraid that they will just get stuck back together again? In any case I continue working on what has become an unpleasant task until to my relief I hear Giovanna say it is time to clean up the room.

Over the course of Bill's first month in the classroom the children drew him more and more into their activities. One day in early March as the children were finishing the morning snack in the hallway outside the classroom Valerio asks, 'Bill di rosa' (Bill say pink). Bill says pink and Valerio says,

'Cacca rosa!' (Poo-poo rosa!). All of the children laugh uproariously at this 'poo-poo' joke. Carlotta now quickly repeats the routine asking Bill to say a different colour with the same resulting laughter and although Bill laughs along with the children, he is also a bit uncomfortable because several teachers are nearby.

We have discussed in earlier work how the mere mention of 'poo-poo' and 'pee-pee' is part of the humour of preschool children (Corsaro, 1985). In this case, the children were not only trying to be funny, but also testing Bill to see how he would react. A few days after this incident, Bill was sitting at a worktable with several children and Renato suddenly jumped up and said, 'Watch Bill.' He then did a little dance and sang his personal version of a famous Italian song: 'Italia si! Italia no! Italia cacca!' (Italy yes! Italy no! Italy poo-poo!). This time Bill was laughing as hard as the other children who witnessed this hilarious performance for in this instance, Renato's performance was funny well beyond the reference to poo-poo.

Bill's experience with the sweets, his helping of the children with the building materials, and his later inclusion in the 'poo-poo' jokes captures a period in which he was part of a range of transitory rituals that adults often must go through to be accepted into the peer world of young children. In the example of the sweets Bill's status as something other than a typical adult was still unclear to the children. Later the children grew accustomed to Bill entering into their play, coming down to their physical level by sitting on the floor with them, and by not directing their activities and intervening in disputes. In the example with the building materials Bill was accepted into the play as a peer, but his adult skill in being able to break apart the tightly wedged blocks was appropriated by the children. The last example of the poo-poo jokes was a test of Bill by the children because adults would often disapprove of such talk as silly and inappropriate. Bill's initial discomfort and then genuinely positive reaction to Renato's creative performance helped him to develop a sense of trust and acceptance in the children's peer culture.

A review of field notes over the first months reveals many other instances where Bill was gradually drawn into the children's activities. On one occasion, Valerio had brought some sunglasses to school and several of the children commented on and asked to wear them. Bill also asked to try them on and when he removed his own glasses to do so, Valerio took them from his hand, put them on and shouted, 'Look I'm wearing Bill's glasses!' Angelo quickly grabbed them from Valerio, put them on, and began stumbling around the room to show that everything now looked blurry through the lenses. Several other children wanted a turn and Bill cautioned them to be careful with the glasses. Eventually Bill got his glasses back and began cleaning away the children's fingerprints with a special cloth he had to polish the plastic lenses. Valerio then asked to use the cloth to clean his sunglasses, embellishing the process by first spitting on the lenses. Although

Bill preferred the dry cleaning method, he did not protest and Valerio asked to use the cloth several other times that day. Later in the day Luciano asked if he could use the cloth to clean his real glasses. Bill said fine but told him there was no need for spit.

In this example we again see how adult researchers can find themselves uneasy in their participation in children's peer culture. Bill had some fear that his glasses could be damaged in the play, and therefore cautioned the children to be careful. Also because the cloth for the glasses was for dry (not wet) cleaning, Bill restricted the use of the spit cleaning method, a restriction which also demonstrates the adult researcher's different view of body excretions compared to that of children.

After his first month at the school Bill noticed in a review of his field notes that most of the children had actively taken notice of him, included him in their play, and even teased him about his poor Italian. Reflecting on the notes he realized, however, that a few children seemed a bit shy around him and one girl in particular, Irene, had not yet spoken to him. This situation was about to change, however, as captured in the following excerpt from field notes taken a few days after his own review.

Example 2
March 7, 1996

This morning we are taking a field trip to see an art exhibit at a museum in the centre of the city. As we leave to go out to the bus I have Valerio's hand. Renato also asks to take my hand, but he then notices that Irene is alone and asks for her hand. Irene refuses, backing away from Renato and the group. As we walk toward the bus, Irene comes up and takes my other hand, Renato then takes Valerio's. Valerio lets go of my hand and Irene and I are left as a pair. When we reach the bus door I let go of Irene's hand as she moves onto the bus and I stand at the door with the teachers as all the children enter. When I get on the bus I see that Irene has saved me a seat next to her and I take it. I am a bit surprised by Irene's interest in me this morning because she is one of a few children who have acted a bit shy of me or at least uninterested in being around me. Now today she seems to have made up her mind to be my partner on the trip. On the bus ride Irene says little, but does tell me about other field trips the group has taken this year when I ask her about them. Throughout our entire time at the museum Irene stays close to me and again sits next to me on the bus ride back to the school. As we enter the school she seems very happy.

A few days after the field trip Bill had to alter his normal observational schedule at the school and spend a Monday at the university in Bologna. When he arrived at the preschool the next Tuesday morning several children ran up to him yelling, 'Hi Bill!' and called out to the others that he had arrived. A few minutes later at snack, Irene was sitting next to Bill and she asked what he did in Bologna. Bill was surprised at this, but then remembered he had told the teachers that he was going to Bologna. From Irene's question Bill took it that she or one of the other children had asked where he was. As Bill was thinking about all this, Irene asked why he went to Bologna and he responded that he had to go and talk to his friends at the university. It was clear that his missing one day of his normal schedule had been noticed by the children, and they had come to see him as part of the everyday routines in their class.[2]

As described earlier, the children quickly picked up on Bill's limited competence in Italian. They laughed at his accent and mispronunciations and took great joy in correcting him. One morning after Bill had been observing in the school for around five weeks the teacher, Giovanna, was reading a chapter of the *Wizard of Oz* to the children. After about ten minutes of reading and discussion, Giovanna was called away to answer a phone call, and so she handed Bill the book, suggesting that he continue reading the story. Aware that it would be a difficult task for Bill, the children yelled and clapped thinking this was a great idea. Bill immediately ran into trouble trying to pronounce the word for 'scarecrow' which in Italian is '*spaventapasseri*'. The children laughed and hooted at his stumbling over this and other words. Some children even fell from their seats in pretend hysterics at his predicament and his problems were made even worse given that there seemed to be a 'scarecrow' in every other sentence. To Bill's relief Giovanna returned and, when asked how he did, the children laughed and said he could not read well. Sandra yelled out, 'We didn't understand anything!' Giovanna then took the book back from Bill, but the children shouted: 'No, we want Bill to read more!' Taking the book back, he struggled through another page amidst animated laughter before handing the book back to Giovanna saying, 'Basta così, adesso' (That's enough for now).

There are two aspects of the children's response to Bill's problems with the language that were different from his earlier experiences in Bologna. First, in Bologna he observed a large mixed age group where there was wide diversity in the children's literacy skills and although the Bolognese children were introduced to reading and writing, it was not a central part of the curriculum. In this group of 5 year olds in Modena, lessons and activities related to reading and writing were now everyday occurrences in these last months of their last year in the preschool. Although they laughed at his errors, they realized Bill could read and they identified with his problems to some degree. Second, the children in Modena were also studying English and they realized that Bill was competent in this foreign language, which was very difficult for them. In short, it was reassuring to them that this new adult in their midst shared some of their same experiences and challenges.

William A. Corsaro and Luisa Molinari

Acceptance and Participant Status with Teachers

Giovanna and Carla, the two main teachers in the classroom we studied, had been working together for over ten years. They were interested in our transition project and expressed an eagerness to participate when we talked with them and the director before Bill began his observations. They were, as any teachers would be in such a situation, sensitive to Bill's presence in their classroom over the first weeks of observation, but were put at ease somewhat by his quick acceptance by the children, his frequent presence and his commitment to experience life in the school from the children's perspective. The teachers noted in interviews at the end of the study that an adult male researcher who sings and dances with the children and gets down on the floor to play with them is not seen as threatening for long. Yet they did wonder what Bill was writing in his notebook and often found his descriptions of what he thought about the activities in their classroom to be a bit vague. In a later interview Giovanna noted that she hesitated at times in raising her voice with the children (a not uncommon occurrence in most Italian classrooms) in Bill's presence. However, she also said that after a few weeks Bill became like a piece of furniture, a taken-for-granted participant in the setting.

Several events that occurred during Bill's first six weeks in the school capture his gradual acceptance as an everyday member of the local culture. The first was his acceptance of the role of '*Mago dei boschi*' (The wizard of the woods) in a play the teachers performed for the children on 20 February, which was Fat Tuesday, the celebration of Carnivale. Bill was aware of the play, *The Lambs and the Wolf*, because he had heard the teachers talking about it and observed them practising for the performance on several occasions. On the day before the scheduled performance Giovanna and Carla had left the classroom for a dress rehearsal while Bill remained in the room with the children during their English lesson. A few minutes later, one of the teachers from the 3-year-old class came in and motioned for Bill to come out to the hallway. She and another teacher from the 4-year-old group asked Bill to be the wizard, noting that the only male in the school (an assistant teacher in the other 5-year-old group) was playing the part of the wolf. Bill saw Giovanna and Carla standing to the side smiling and surmised that they had volunteered him for the role. He was assured he would have no lines to speak and had only to tap the dead wolf (who was slain for his misdeeds by the lambs' mother) with a magic wand. Bill quickly accepted and a few minutes later successfully carried out his limited role in the rehearsal, receiving a loud ovation from all the teachers.

On several occasions the teachers delighted in testing and teasing Bill about his problems with Italian. This testing sometimes occurred when the children included Bill in various learning activities. In one instance the children were shown several objects. The objects were then put in a bag and the children were asked to reach in without looking, select an object and identify it. The children enjoyed this task and after every child had had a turn, Carla asked Bill to reach in the bag. She knew of course that he could easily identify the objects, but she also knew that he might not know the Italian word for many of them. Bill got hold of a can opener and immediately realized he was in trouble. He stuttered a little and then said in Italian, 'It's a thing to open things.' Carla and Giovanna laughed loudly and one child, Sandra, who was always quick to pass judgement, shouted: '*Ma Bill è una apriscatole!*' (But Bill it's a can opener!).

In a final example the children were having an English lesson in which they were attempting to learn the song 'Twinkle, Twinkle, Little Star' in English. The English teacher first had the whole group of children sing the song in Italian and then went through it line by line with them in English. He then divided the children into groups of four and asked them to sing the song in English, assigning a grade from 1 to 10 for their performance. Although Bill thought the children did pretty well, the English teacher, Joseph, was a tough grader and no group scored above a 4. After each group had had a turn, Giovanna suggested that Bill sing the song in English. He did so perfectly and Joseph gave him a 10. 'Now sing it in Italian,' requested Giovanna. Bill pleaded to have the children sing it again so he could listen closely and they did so. Bill started out pretty well in his Italian rendition, but stumbled over several words, stopping after two lines. Giovanna and the children laughed loudly and Joseph shouted out Bill's grade: '*Sotto zero!*' (Below zero!).

Overall, these examples involving the teachers, like earlier ones when the children teased and tested Bill, capture the subtle ways in which the ethnographer and participants collectively define and produce the ethnographer's participant status in the local cultures of the research setting. Language is often a particular arena for this collective process, with the lack of full linguistic competence working against the frequently perceived higher status of the ethnographer in a positive way such that it enables informants and participants to test, to reflect on, and to develop more fully their cross-cultural relationship with the ethnographer.

Becoming an Active Member of the Group

After field entry and acceptance into the 5-year-old group, Bill became a regular participant in everyday and special activities and in this section we reflect on Bill's evolving membership in the group.

Participating in Everyday Routines

After several weeks in the school Bill found that he was often invited into play activities by the children. Consider Example 3.

Example 3
March 4 Free Play Outside

After meeting time the children start free play inside the school, but it is a nice day and Giovanna says they can go outside if they like. Some children go to get their coats as an assistant teacher, Patriza, is going outside with them. Renato asks me to come out, so I go to get my coat. When I get outside I see that it is mainly boys who have come out. They are climbing in the bars and running around. At one point Dario, Renato, and Valerio gather some sticks and place them on the ground under the climbing bars. They protect their sticks from the others. There is then some discussion of fire, and I suggest that Indians start fires by rubbing sticks together. Renato and Valerio decide to try this, but Dario says I do not know what I am talking about and it won't work. Several other boys join us and they all now begin to gather grass and leaves and place them with the sticks. They start to stir the leaves with the sticks and Dario says they are making salad. Shortly after this we are called back inside by Giovanna.

In this example Bill is invited into the play and at one point suggests an activity relevant to the ongoing activity. He is by no means given any special status in the play and, in fact, Dario rejects Bill's claim about being able to start fire with the sticks. Another example captures the children drawing Bill into their artistic activities.

Example 4
March 5 Painting

Giovanna and Carla were working on an art activity with seven children. The work was in line with a long term project involving the children's thinking about light and dark, and it involved each child selecting a picture of a sunrise or sunset which had been clipped from a magazine. They then pasted the picture onto a larger sheet of art paper. The next step was to mix the colours and paint the blank page so that it blended with the magazine picture in the middle. Giovanna and Carla joked with each other encouraging the children who were working with the opposite teacher to select the more demanding magazine pictures. I was very impressed with the teachers' patience in their instructing the children on how to match the colours and the children's paintings. Despite the complex subtleties of many of the purple, pink, and violet hues of the sunrises and sunsets, it was very difficult to even discern the embedded magazine pictures in many of the children's paintings. Having little artistic ability I felt very inadequate watching this activity. I was also envious of the children, begrudging the limited exposure I had had to art as a child. Later I moved over to another part of the room where Luciano and Sandra were painting with water colours. This was '*disegno libero*' (free painting) and was less complex than the project work. Yet the pictures the children were painting were very impressive. They had drawn houses, trees, flowers, grass, etc. in outline with a pencil and now were painting them in. They also used Kleenex to blot the paint on in some instances, creating a nice effect. They had surely been shown this trick by the teachers. I tell the children I am not so good at painting and did not go to preschool. Luciano says, 'But Bill it's easy!' He hands me a brush and instructs me to paint a small section of grass at the bottom of his picture. I accept this offer willingly and do a good job. But it is only a bit of grass – I could not produce a painting like Luciano's or Sandra's even with a good deal of practice.

We can see from this example the easy acceptance of Bill by the teachers and children – the teachers joking with one another demonstrated their high degree of comfort in going about their work in his presence. It was also apparent that Luciano and Sandra did not see Bill's admission of incompetence in painting as remarkable. Rather comfortable in their own everyday artistic work of this type, they easily included him into the activity.

Certification as a Member of Group 5b

As we discussed earlier, the group that Bill observed in the *scuola dell'infanzia* was one of two 5-year-old groups and there was also a group of 4 and 3 year olds. Given that the 5 year olds had been at the school for nearly three years, these children and their parents were very well known by all the teachers and many of the younger children. Thus, Bill was part of one of the most high-status and visible groups in the school.

Bill's group was known as the 5bs. After only a few days at the school, he noticed that both the teachers and the children in the other groups came to see him as a member of the 5bs. The 5b children certainly helped with this association. In situations when children from the various groups came together for joint activities children from the 5b group would often call out: 'Bill belongs to us!' The children were also very sensitive to the correct pronunciation of Bill's first name. There was some tendency on the part of children from the other groups and other teachers to refer to Bill as 'Billy', thus transforming his name to fit the common Italian pattern of names ending in a vowel sound. The children especially relished correcting the music teacher and a substitute teacher in the 5b class who frequently made this error with the admonishment: 'Non Billy, Bill!'

The following example of the 'grass war' captures a dramatic confirmation of Bill's membership as one of the 5bs.

Example 5
April 18 *La Guerra Dell'Erba* (The Grass War)

The outside yard has been freshly mowed with cut grass lying all around. Some of the girls (Elisa, Carlotta, and Michela) begin gathering the grass and take it to an area under the climbing structure where they make a bed. At one point, Michela and then others lie down on the bed and say: 'Che Morbido!' (How soft it is!). Several other girls enter the play, but Elisa, Carlotta, and Michela control the activity. The new recruits are allowed to bring grass, but not place it on the bed.

Later Carlotta, returns to say that one of the boys from the other 5-year-old group at the school hit her while she was gathering grass. The other girls become upset and decide to go get the boy. The girls march over carrying grass, come up behind the boy, and pummel him with the grass. The girls then run back to the climbing structure and celebrate their revenge – especially Carlotta who is all smiles. Eventually the boy gets a few of his friends and they come by and throw grass at the girls. The girls chase after the boys who are outnumbered and take the worst of it in another exchange of grass throwing.

The grass war now escalates with girls and boys on both sides becoming involved. In fact, all but a few of the 5-year-old group (5b) I am observing are now in the grass war. The war continues for some time until Marina suggests to the children in our group that they make peace. Marina with several children behind her marches up to the boy who hit Carlotta and offers her hand in peace. The boy responds by throwing grass in Marina's face. Marina returns to the group, and Carlotta says: 'They don't want peace!' But Marina says she will try again. The second time she offers her hand the boy throws grass again, but over the objections of another boy who is in his group. Marina stands her ground after being hit with the grass. The second boy pulls his friend aside and suggests they make peace. The other boy is against the proposal, but eventually agrees and the two then shake hands with Marina. Marina then returns to our group and declares: 'Peace has been established!' The two groups now meet for a round of handshaking. I also exchange handshakes with the kids from the other 5-year-old group who identify me as part of the opposing group.

In this episode the children from 5b appropriate objects from the adult world and use them to create an innovative pretend play routine, a creative activity which gives the children a shared sense of control over their social environment. The intergroup conflict between the two 5-year-old groups is both related to, and further develops, the strong solidarity within the 5b group and later the peace negotiation, symbolically marked by handshakes, demonstrates the children's awareness of a sense of community in the school. Bill's inclusion in the handshakes confirmed his place in this community.[3]

Participating in Special Events

Bill's participation extended to joining in the preparations for and activities during grandparents' day and the two visits to the elementary school, both of which occurred in May, and culminated in the end-of-the-year school party in late June, an event which was always eagerly anticipated by the children and parents. However, this year's party was even more special because it would mark the end of the children's and their families' time at the school. Preparations occurred on two fronts. A small group of the most active parents encouraged all the children's parents, siblings and grandparents to attend, enlisted volunteers to order and serve pizza and other refreshments, and collected funds to purchase gifts for the teachers. In the school the teachers and children were also busy. The teachers constructed small diplomas for the children and worked with the children on a group portrait. The last project involved the children drawing individual self-portraits which were then pasted on to a large group picture. The teachers then made a photocopy of the group picture and had it printed on tee shirts for the children, teachers and Bill, who were all to wear these shirts at the end-of-the-year party.

The children also practised several dances that they were to perform at the party and in these Bill had a key role because one of the songs danced to was a favourite of many American children, 'The Hokey Pokey.' Because the words were in English it was Bill's job to repeat the words while demonstrating the appropriate movements in the dance. The children and teachers loved this. Not only is it very funny to hear someone say and see someone put their backside (and many other body parts) in and shake them all around, to the children it was especially funny to see Bill doing this. Additionally, one of the teachers, Carla, continually made an error in pronouncing 'Hokey Pokey' as 'Honky Tonky'. Bill corrected her, trying to explain as best he could in Italian that Honky Tonky was a particular genre of music. Carla thought that he was just correcting her pronunciation. This incident is interesting because it was a reversal of roles: the teachers often had to correct Bill's Italian. He realized now that some of their corrections no doubt also went beyond mere pronunciation.

The big night of the party arrived. The children, teachers and Bill showed off their tee shirts, the parents loved the dancing (especially the Hokey Pokey), the children received their diplomas, and the pizza was great. The parents presented the teachers with very elegant wrist watches and they generously gave Bill a beautiful beach towel. After the ceremonies, gifts

William A. Corsaro and Luisa Molinari

and pizza everyone played games. The first thing the parents wanted to try was the Hokey Pokey!

Identifying and Participating in Priming Events

Earlier we discussed the concept of interpretive reproduction. We argued that this perspective stresses the importance of children's participation in collective processes with adults and peers in the local cultures which signify that one is part of a group. In these, certain cultural practices and routines prepare or prime members for future changes. Priming events – as we propose to call them – involve collective activities in which children, by their very participation, attend prospectively to ongoing or anticipated changes in their lives. Priming events are crucial to children's social construction of representations of temporal aspects of their lives (including important life transitions) because children's social representations do not arise from simply thinking about social life, but rather through their collective, practical activities with others (Corsaro 1990, 1997). In the *scuola dell'infanzia* we documented both formal priming events in which the children were clearly conscious of how the activities were related to their coming transitions to first grade and subtle priming events where awareness was less apparent as the activities were embedded in recurrent routines in the preschool (Corsaro et al. 1998). Here we briefly consider some direct and other more subtle priming events in both the school and peer culture and their importance when conducting research with children.

Priming in the Preschool Curriculum

The most obvious priming events in the school curriculum for the children's transition to elementary school were the planned group visits in May to the nearby elementary school. Bill accompanied the children and teacher on two visits to the school. The first visit involved inspecting the art, science and music labs, the playground area, the gymnasium and the cafeteria. In the second visit the fifth grade teachers took the children to their classrooms. In September the children would join one of four new first grade groups that would be taught by the fifth grade teachers. In this way they got to meet their teachers and see their future classrooms. However, what was most interesting about visiting the fifth grade classrooms was how excited the fifth graders were. The big children took the preschoolers under their wings and took them to their desks, showed them their work, and told them all about their class and their teachers. The preschoolers loved all this attention from the older children and, in turn, the older children experienced these visits as a priming event preparing them for leaving school and the teachers with whom they had been working for the past five years.

One point we want to stress here is that the school visits served as priming events not only for the children, but for the researchers as well. Although arrangements had been made for our future research in the elementary school by Luisa in a prior meeting with the principal, we had not yet met the teachers or visited their classrooms. Thus, in these visits Bill, together with the children, met the school principal, the children's future first grade teachers, and became familiar with the classrooms and activities. During the visits he shared with the children a glimpse of their future schooling and the next phase of our longitudinal ethnography.

Priming in the Peer Culture

Although adults and children are often consciously aware of their participation in priming events, as we saw in our earlier discussion of the school culture, some priming activities have more subtle effects. In the peer culture these are often embedded in recurrent routines in which the focus is on peer concerns and values. In the following example we see how priming occurs in peer discussion and debate and the involvement of the researcher in these routines.

Example 6
April 2 The Hair Debate

A debate develops between Marina and Sandra. Sandra insists a doll with little hair (an infant) must be a boy because it has short hair. Marina disagrees and says when children are babies sometimes both boys and girls have short hair. But Sandra disputes this claim, and some children side with Marina and some with Sandra. Marina then points to the shelf where the children's personal books (which document the children's time in the school) are stored and asks me to reach up and get hers down. She says 'Grazie Bill,' as I hand her the book. She then turns to a page where there is a picture of her when she was about one year old and she does not have much hair. 'See,' she says to Sandra, 'this is me and I had short hair then.' Sandra now says, 'Hai ragione' (You are right), and the issue is settled.

Marina's use of Bill in this episode is interesting because she relies only on his size, which enabled him to get the book down. She did not ask Bill for support for her position and did not assume he knew any more than the children about the disputed topic. Theoretically, the episode is very interesting in several respects. It shows how the children take an element of the adult school culture – the existence of these books that they have created about their experiences in the school over the three years – and use it to address an issue in the peer culture.

Subtle priming events also occur within peer culture when children spontaneously practise and evaluate literacy skills introduced in school projects (like those related to the *Wizard of Oz* we discussed earlier) in everyday peer activities. For example, in the last several weeks of school, the children would frequently print words (most especially their names and names of friends) into their drawings during *disegno libero*. They would also evaluate each other's skills (especially pointing out errors) and, on occasion, challenge each other to come up with new words or to write in cursive.

About this same time, however, the children also began to ask Bill to print things into the notebook he used to record field observations. The children were very aware of this book and in the first weeks often asked to see it and sometimes draw pictures in it. In the last six weeks or so, they frequently printed their names or certain words with their drawings. Consider Example 7.

Example 7
June 6 Printing Names

I am sitting at a table with Renato, Luciano, and Dario who are drawing pictures. Marina comes and joins us. She colours my hand with a purple marker and then she prints my first and last name in my notebook: BILL (in blue) CORSARO (in green) . . . Carlotta now joins the group and prints my name in my notebook. Stefania then comes over and prints my name under where Carlotta has printed it and then she prints her first and last name. Valerio then joins us and prints the number 20 and his first name and his companion Angelo prints 21 and his first name. It looks like the following:

BILL
CORSARO
BILL
CARLOTTA
DANATO
20 VALERIO
21
ANGELO

In a final example the children go beyond printing their names to composing a short letter.

Example 8
June 14 A Letter for Luciano's Little Sister

I am sitting at a worktable with Luciano, Stefania and several other children. Luciano is printing a letter to his sister. Stefania tells me to write what Luciano is doing in my notebook. So I do so in Italian and show it to her:

Luciano scrive una lettera per la sua sorellina. ('Luciano is writing a letter for his little sister').

Luciano then suggests that Stefania also write a letter to his sister which she does with Luciano's help. It reads:

CARA LUISA,

TANTI BACIONI DA STEFANIA LUCIANO E DA BILL. (Many big kisses from Stefania Luciano and from Bill.)

These examples nicely capture how literacy activities first presented in teacher directed tasks are appropriated and used by the children in their peer culture. Furthermore, the children document these priming activities directly into Bill's notebook. We see here an excellent example of research *with* rather than *on* children which is similar to research by Mayall and by Alderson (reported on in Chapters 6 and 12). Finally, this documentation by children of data directly relevant to our research interests demonstrates the value of longitudinal ethnography. It is the result of our acceptance, participation and evolving membership in the school and peer cultures.

Conclusion

In this chapter we have discussed our use of longitudinal ethnography in further developing our theoretical perspective of interpretive reproduction. In a seminal set of articles on qualitative methods the sociologist Howard Becker (1970) discussed the theoretical and methodological importance of formally documenting the history of the research process in ethnographic studies. Such documentation importantly integrates doing, rendering, and interpreting ethnographic research. All too often methodological discussions are separated from practice as discussions of data collection and analysis strategies including reliability, validity, and more recently the writing (or narrative rendering) of ethnography are abstracted away from the actual doing of ethnographic research (Clifford and Marcus 1986; Denzin and Lincoln 1994; Hammersley 1992) including the ethnographic study of children and youth (Fine and Sandstrom 1988; Waksler, 1991). We have stayed very close to the practice of our longitudinal, comparative ethno-graphic research with young children to demonstrate how this practice was directly related to the development and extension of our theoretical perspective of interpretive reproduction.

From the perspective of interpretive reproduction, socialization is not something that happens to children; it is a process in which children, in interaction with others, produce their own peer culture and eventually come to reproduce, to extend and to join the adult world (Corsaro 1992: 175). Interpretive reproduction is made up of three types of collective actions: children's creative appropriation of information and knowledge from the adult world; children's production and participation in a series of peer cultures; and children's contribution to the reproduction and extension of the adult culture. These activities follow a certain progression in that appropriation enables cultural production, which contributes to reproduction and change. The activities are, however, not historically partitioned. Instead these collective actions occur both within the moment and over time (Corsaro 1997: 41).

Thus, it is crucial to study interpretive reproduction longitudinally, as a process of children's evolving membership in their culture in the manner described in this chapter. We have shown how in a group of Italian preschool children, we were accepted and defined by them, and then with the children participated in events which prepared or primed them for their coming transition to elementary school. These priming events involved activities that were both iterative (embedded in ongoing routines in the school and peer cultures) and projective (creative, often semi-conscious glimpses into the future). In such priming events social actors are 'immersed in a temporal flow' during which 'they move "beyond themselves" into the future and construct changing images of where they think they are going, where they want to go, and how they can get there from where they are at present' (Emirbayer and Mische 1998: 984).

As ethnographers we experienced and documented not only these priming events, but also in some cases how we were appropriated by the children and teachers to take on active roles in the collective production of the events themselves. Finally, in some cases we were instructed by the children on which priming events to record in our notes (e.g. by Stefania to record Luciano's writing of a letter to his sister), and in other instances had the notebook and pen taken from our hands as the children recorded the priming events themselves. Thus, we actively entered (or were appropriated into) the temporal flow of interpretive reproduction and were primed with the children to move from the preschool to first grade. And that is exactly what we did. But a reflection and discussion of that transition is another story.

Notes

1 During the research we met twice a week to reflect on and discuss the ongoing research, in addition to the joint accomplishment of more practical research tasks. These twice weekly meetings provided opportunities for evaluating Bill's reactions to events he observed in the field, discussing ideas about data collection strategies, analysing observational and interview data, and generating and discussing initial interpretations. Our collaboration on this longitudinal, comparative

ethnography continues. Overall, we found that our different cultural backgrounds and research experience enriched the quality of this collaborative ethnography.

2 Although Irene's behaviour can be interpreted in a number of ways, given our knowledge of her, which has developed over the course of this study, we believe that she was shy and used the field trip as a means for acting on her growing interest in Bill. Having established a closer bond with Bill, she was then curious (and perhaps somewhat disappointed) about the change in his schedule.

3 Although Bill's inclusion in the peace-making phase of this example clearly demonstrates his membership in the 5b group, his actual participation in the activity fits his general status as a peripheral participant in the children's activities (Corsaro 1985). While his actual level of participation varied over time and across events, Bill refrained from initiating or terminating episodes; repairing disrupted activity; or settling disputes. What he did do was try to play (or take part in the school culture more generally) without dramatically affecting the nature or flow of activities. In this instance given his adult status (even though he was seen as an atypical adult), Bill could not actively enter into the grass war (e.g. 'throw grass', 'shout at and run after children') without dramatically affecting the play. However, given his participant status Bill did not attempt to stop the grass war and may have faced some serious choices if the play became overly physical. In such a case Bill's relationship with the teachers and children would have allowed him to signal for help if needed and he would, of course, have actively intervened in the play to protect a child from injury.

References

Becker, H. (1970) *Sociological Work: Method and Substance*, New Brunswick, NJ: Transaction Books.

Berentzen, S. (1995) 'Boyfriend–girlfriend relationships as social organization: a studying of the growth and decline of "Go-With" relationships in a Black ghetto', unpublished paper.

Clifford, J. and Marcus, G. (1986) *Writing Culture: The Poetics and Politics of Ethnography*, Berkeley, CA: University of California Press.

Corsaro, W. (1985) *Friendship and Peer Culture in the Early Years*, Norwood, NJ: Ablex.

Corsaro, W. (1992) 'Interpretive reproduction in children's peer cultures', *Social Psychology Quarterly* 55: 160–77.

Corsaro, W. (1993) 'Interpretive reproduction in children's role play', *Childhood* 1: 64–74.

Corsaro, W. (1996) 'Transitions in early childhood: the promise of comparative, longitudinal ethnography', in R. Jessor, A. Colby and R. Shweder (eds) *Ethnography and Human Development*, Chicago: University of Chicago Press.

Corsaro, W. (1997) *The Sociology of Childhood*, Thousand Oaks, CA: Pine Forge Press.

Corsaro, W. and Molinari, L. (1990) 'From seggiolini to discussione: the generation and extension of peer culture among Italian preschool children', *International Journal of Qualitative Studies in Education* 3: 213–30.

Corsaro, W., Molinari, L. and Zetti, S. (1998) 'Interpretive reproduction and priming events: children's transition from preschool to elementary school in Italy', unpublished manuscript.

Denzin, N. and Lincoln, Y. (1994) *Handbook of Qualitative Research*, Thousand Oaks, CA: Sage.

Edwards, C., Gandini, L. and Forman, G. (eds) (1993) *The Hundred Languages of Children*, Norwood, NJ: Ablex.

Emirbayer, M. and Mische, A. (1998) 'What is agency?', *American Journal of Sociology* 103: 962–1023.

Fine, G. and Sandstrom, K. (1988) *Knowing Children: Participant Observation with Minors*, Newbury Park, CA: Sage.

Gandini, L. (1993) 'Fundamentals of the Reggio Emilia approach to early childhood education', *Young Children* 49: 73–7.

Hammersley, M. (1992) *What's Wrong with Ethnography?*, London: Routledge.

Lave, J. and Wenger, E. (1991) *Situated Learning: Legitimate Peripheral Participation*, New York: Cambridge University Press.

Mandell, N. (1988) 'The least-adult role in studying children', *Journal of Contemporary Ethnography* 16: 433–67.

Molinari, L. and Corsaro, W. (1994) 'La genesi e l'evoluzione della cultura dei bambini', *Bambini* X(5): 38–45.

Rizzo, T., Corsaro, W. and Bates, J. (1992) 'Ethnographic methods and interpretive analysis: expanding the methodological options of psychologists', *Developmental Review* 12: 101–23.

Schatzman, L. and Strauss, A. (1973) *Field Research: Strategies for a Natural Sociology*, Englewood Cliffs, NJ: Prentice Hall.

Waksler, F. (ed.) (1991). *Studying the Social Worlds of Children: Sociological Readings*, London: Falmer Press.

Wulff, H. (1988) *Twenty Girls: Growing Up, Ethnicity and Excitement in a South London Microculture*, Stockholm: University of Stockholm.

10 Learning the Lives of Disabled Children

Developing a Reflexive Approach

John Davis, Nick Watson and
Sarah Cunningham-Burley

Introduction

This chapter discusses research which has been carried out at one location, that of a special school for children with multiple impairments in Scotland.[1] It describes the process through which one member of the research team (John) with support from others on the team (Nick and Sarah) developed a reflexive approach which enabled him to interact with a number of children who employed a variety of forms of verbal and non-verbal communication.[2] It illustrates that the reflexive process requires children's researchers to explore their preconceptions concerning children's cultures.

Initially we discuss the reflexive approach and describe our academic leanings concerning childhood research and disability studies. This precedes an illustration of the processes through which our prior understandings were questioned at different times during the fieldwork. Specifically we focus on how John's entry into the field, the processes through which he learned the children's languages and the variety of research roles he adopted within the school provided him with numerous opportunities both to learn about the children he worked with and to question his own and other academic understandings of childhood.

Reflexivity

Central to current ethnographic approach is the use of reflexivity. But what is reflexivity? An honest answer to this question might be that it is something easier to do than to define. However, some writers do provide valuable assistance for those attempting to resolve this question. Callaway (1992) tells us that reflexivity opens the way to a more radical consciousness of self, that it is a mode of self-analysis and political awareness. Hertz (1997), in agreement, suggests that reflexivity is achieved 'through detachment, internal dialogue and constant (and intensive) scrutiny' of the process through which researchers construct and question their interpretations of field experiences (Hertz 1997: vii).[3]

This approach requires ethnographers to put their preconceptions and prejudices to fruitful use (Okely 1975; Campbell 1995). How people respond to the ethnographer's presence is examined in order that ethnographers can learn about the differences between their cultures and the cultures of those they study (Hammersley and Atkinson 1983; Okely 1975; Wax 1971; Agar 1980). That is, ethnographers learn about others by comparing their own values to those of the people they interact with (Campbell 1995; Marcus and Fischer 1986; Geertz 1973).

In sociology it has been argued that the engagement of researcher and subject is a meeting of two languages (the meta-language of the sociologist and the everyday language of those being studied) and that this requires sociologists to question how their academic knowledge influences their interpretations of others (Giddens 1976). However, this position does not take account of the personal culture of the researcher. That is, it does not emphasize the fact that the way that researchers communicate with people and react to the everyday occurrences of the research setting is in some way dependent on the values they have acquired, which may have little to do with academia, during their life course.

We believe there to be at least two languages at work in the heads of ethnographers. The first is the language/culture of their academic paradigm, the second the everyday language/culture based on the ethnographer's personal history. Therefore, ethnographers should question the influence of both their academic and personal preconceptions on the processes of interpretation. This means there is no separation between fieldwork and analysis, personal interpretations and academic theories are scrutinized at the same time (Okely 1994).

This process can include ethnographers explaining how they gain the knowledge held within their final text (Prat 1986) and their own relationship to events they portray (Crapanzano 1986). This approach is neither 'navel gazing' nor 'narcissism', rather it enables the reader to understand the ethnographer's experiences within the context of an ever changing and fluid research setting (Okely 1992).

In this project the reflexive process took place both in the field, as John interacted with people in a variety of situations and in the office when we, as a team, discussed John's experiences.[4] This occurred on a daily basis over the phone and during our weekly meetings where we considered his field notes. Opportunities were provided to question interpretation when reporting back to the research team. Analysis of the field notes was shared between the members of the research team. Team work reinforced the rigorous nature of the ethnographic process – not only did the ethnographer have to question his own interpretations but also he had to take account of the interpretations of the research team.

As part of this process the academic preconceptions we held prior to the fieldwork became evident and we were forced to reconsider our own beliefs. Before discussing this process we shall outline what those academic positions were in terms of literature on childhood and disability studies.[5] We have chosen to separate out our writings on childhood and disability because as Shakespeare and Watson (1998) and Priestley (1998) have demonstrated, there is very little cross over between the two paradigms. That is, very few writers within the paradigm of the new sociology of childhood write about disabled children's lives and very few writers in the field of disability studies display an interest in writing about children's lives. Indeed, we attempt to overcome this division in our conclusion.

Exploring our Preconceptions about Children's Cultures

The research team came from quite different academic backgrounds. We had a range of knowledge covering interpretative sociology, disability research, ethnographic work with children, social anthropology, education, social policy, sociology of the family and medical sociology. Despite our different starting points we discovered that we carried with us similar ideas about what the project was about.

From a childhood research perspective we wished to approach this study from the position that children are social actors in their own right who create their own cultures which are as complex as adult cultures (Wartofsky 1983; Tammivaara and Enright 1986; Hardman 1973). We believed that their voices have a right to be heard and taken account of as enshrined in Article 12 of the UN Convention on Rights of the Child (Morrow and Richards 1996). Through our previous research we were aware of the ethical considerations, the variety of research roles and the plethora of research tools which might be employed to work with children and enable their voices to become evident. However, we believed that these techniques could not be applied universally to all children and therefore, that they should be questioned reflexively during the research process (our position is outlined with regard to other authors elsewhere: see Davis 1998).

Implicit in our preconceptions was the notion that children understand the rules of social behaviour (Mackay 1991) and that they are mature competent people capable of offering the researcher their views (Alderson 1995). We did not expect to find one single type of child in the school we were visiting. That is, we questioned universal representations of childhood (Opie and Opie 1969, 1991) on the basis that our research topic involved a group of children often represented as 'different'.

We did not want to follow the practices of a number of writers who appeared to predefine groups of children on the basis of social structural categories such as age, race, gender, social class, etc. (e.g. Mauthner 1997; Mayall 1994; Hallden 1994; Hendry et al. 1993). Our feeling was that this body of work took for granted the importance of these categories at the expense of understanding how children of the same age, class, gender or race might exhibit different everyday behaviour (Thorne 1993).

We did not want to begin with pre-set sociological categories in our minds, rather we hoped to differentiate between children in terms of their everyday experiences. This aim was strengthened by the work of a small number of authors who have been able to illustrate, from children's own perspectives, a variety of different childhoods (e.g. Levin 1994; Glauser 1990; Ritala-Koskinen 1994).[6]

However, we were aware that children's lives did not occur in a socio-logical void (Qvortrup 1994; James et al. 1998); we were interested to under-stand the structural influences on children's everyday lives within the context that:

> Childhood and children's social relationships and cultures are worthy of study in their own right and not just in respect to their social construc-tion by adults. This means that children must be seen as actively involved in the construction of their own social lives, the lives of those around them and of the societies in which they live. They can no longer be regarded as simply the passive subjects of structural determinations.
>
> (James and Prout 1990: 6)

There was no doubt in our mind that children are active and capable of making their own choices (Brannen and O'Brian 1995; James and Prout 1990) and that they behaved as highly skilled and flexible social actors (James and Prout 1995). Here, we also drew from Bourdieu's idea of habitus:

> It is in the relationship between the two capacities which define the habi-tus, the capacity to produce classifiable practices and words, and the capacity to differentiate and appreciate those practices and products (taste), that the represented social world i.e., the space of life styles, is constituted.
>
> (Bourdieu 1986: 17)

Bourdieu suggests that social identity is defined and asserted through differ-ence and that individuals and groups recognize how they are different from other individuals and groups. He indicates that the perception of difference involves a dialectic between conditions of existence (based on the distribu-tion of capital) and habitus (the capacity to produce and appreciate prac-tices). He argues that not only is it possible to differentiate people on a structural level in terms of economic capital but also different groups attri-bute cultural capital to certain behaviour and that they vie to impose their definition of which social phenomena constitute legitimate behaviour (see Davis 1996 for an explanation of this concept in relation to children's participation in sport and physical education).

Bourdieu's idea of habitus has been interpreted as a process of socialization and cultural reproduction (James et al. 1998). However, if we accept the position of James et al. (1998) that children are capable of transforming cultural and social relations, then Bourdieu's notion of habitus becomes less rigid, allowing the possibility that children's social worlds are characterized by constant cultural and social negotiation.

This suggested to us that the social world we were about to enter could be fluid (Thorne 1993) and that this fluidity, in part, could relate to the manner in which different groups interacted. Here, we built on the belief that, at the heart, childhood culture is 'a form of social action contextualised by the many different ways in which children choose to engage with the social institutions and structures that shape the form and process of their everyday lives' (James et al. 1998: 88) and the idea that children are not simply involved in cultural reproduction characterized by mimicry. Indeed, an important focus of our research involved investigating if and when children's lives involved conflict. This, from a childhood research perspective, was one starting point of our study. However, as suggested earlier, we also had a starting-off point in terms of disability research.

Disability and Childhood

We were conscious that there were similarities between Piagetian notions of the naturally developing child (see James and Prout 1990; James et al. 1995) and the ideas prominent within the medicalization of childhood (Shakespeare and Watson 1998). Both notions pathologize children who do not achieve universal standardized developmental targets and identify disability with impairment. They show little awareness of the possibility that these concepts are socially and culturally defined. As a consequence, academic research has been preoccupied with differentiating children on the basis of their impairments, 'measuring children's bodies and minds against physical and cognitive norms' (Priestley 1998: 208–9) and providing advice from a medical and developmental perspective about good practice for working with children with specific impairments.

Since the mid-1970s disabled people have fought to change medically led definitions of disability by arguing that disability is socially constituted, the product of exclusionary practices within society (e.g. Finkelstein 1975; UPIAS/Disability Alliance 1976). This perspective is now known as the 'social model' and has been promoted by many authors (Abberley 1987; Oliver 1990; Morris 1991; Barnes 1991; Zarb 1995). Its benefit for our project was that, in highlighting the social factors that lead to disability, it enabled us to move beyond notions of disabled children as medically defined unchanging individuals.

However, we were concerned about the relevance of the social model of disability as discussed by Oliver (1990) and Barnes (1991) when compared to writings on the new sociology of childhood. First, by defining disability as materially determined (caused by structure) the social model of disability does not incorporate an understanding that disabled children may be capable of affecting the structures surrounding their lives. Second, by promoting a universal concept of disability which suggests that the problems that disabled people encounter can be addressed by structural changes which recognizes their rights as citizens and renegotiates existing power relations, it homogenizes disabled people. If these ideas were applied to the study of disabled children, we were concerned that the outcome could be that the fluid and diverse nature of their lives might be overlooked (Shakespeare and Watson 1998).

We wished to avoid this eventuality because the voices of disabled children have rarely been heard in previous research or they have emerged only in studies preoccupied with issues of care and characterized by narratives of dependence, vulnerability and exclusion (Shakespeare and Watson 1998; Priestley 1998). Such studies tend to describe disabled children as a homogeneous grouping, make much of the link between disability and poverty, yet only rarely discuss issues such as gender (Humphries and Gordon 1992; Lewis 1995; Middleton 1996; Norwich 1997; Priestley 1998).

The picture is painted of a homogeneous 'disabled child' who is often denied the same rights and choices as other children (Morris 1997), a 'disabled child' who is under constant surveillance (Alan 1996) and cut off from the opportunities to interact socially in the same way as other non-disabled children. Parents, the medical profession and local authority officials are heavily implicated in this process, especially with regard to the type of education (special or mainstream) the disabled child receives (Tomlinson and Colquhoun 1995; Middleton 1996; Norwich 1997; Alderson and Goodey 1998). A serious critique has been raised that disabled children are prevented from developing social skills and self-confidence because their lives are controlled by other people (Morris 1997; Norwich 1997; Alderson and Goodey 1998). Though there is much evidence to support these perspectives, they are generalizations of children's lives which do not investigate disabled children's capacities to develop complex and multiple identities (Priestley 1998). Indeed they show little awareness of characterizations of childhood which, as was set out in the previous section, illustrate that children are social actors (James et al. 1998; James and Prout 1990) or that groups of children often characterized as homogeneous entities are likely to have differences within (Thorne 1993).

There are only a few works which succeed in overcoming the unitary notion of the disabled child. For example, Norwich (1997) points out that disabled children by using different strategies are able to both ignore the negative influences on their lives and to challenge negative stereotypes of themselves. Writers such as Thomas (1978), Lewis (1995), Middleton (1996), Morris (1997), Norwich (1997) and Alderson and Goodey (1998) do make attempts to differentiate between disabled children/childhoods by way of social structural categories such as race, class and gender rather than by impairment, however, these studies, again, simply create new homogenized groupings of disabled and fall into the trap discussed earlier and illustrated by Thorne (1993), of failing to understand differences within groups of children of the same, class, gender or race.

For us then, there was a need to investigate the process of disabled children's lives, to investigate whether children who have experience of the same institutions, impairment, regime of care, therapy and so on subscribe to different values or react, on a daily basis, in different ways to the same situations.

The above literature would act as the theoretical position which would be critically reviewed throughout the research process – the academic preconceptions which would be questioned through reflexivity. In no way does this stance relate to the suggestion of Hammersley (1990) that theory developed elsewhere should be tested through ethnography. Our concern here is to follow through our early observations concerning reflexivity by making our academic preconceptions obvious so that our readers can follow how these emerged and were challenged during the ethnographic process.

The ethnographic process not only involves the analysing of one's preconceptions, but also includes, as suggested earlier, the reflexive analysis of the process of gaining access, the roles and research tools employed by the ethnographer and the ethical problems which arise while conducting an ethnography. By illustrating this process we demonstrate the need for researchers to be innovative within and sensitive to a research setting which is full of contradictory expectations and pressures. We shall argue (as Davis 1996, 1998 argued), that the diversity of children's lives can be explored by ethnographers being reflexive about how different children respond to issues of access, the ethnographers role and the research tools they employ. Though we shall be discussing the research process as it occurred with disabled children in a single special school we believe that our experiences and conclusions about research techniques may be applied to other interpretative settings which might include research with disabled and non-disabled adults and children.

Entry into the Field

At the beginning of the project it was imagined that John, the ethnographer, would spend six to eight weeks in this school prior to visiting some of the children in their home locations. However, despite his previous experience of working with children, John found his initial entry into the school extremely difficult which related to his lack of experience working with disabled children. Problems concerning how to communicate with the children led us to extend the time being spent in the school to almost five months, as is outlined in John's field notes below:

> After a very friendly meeting with the head teacher, I was thrown in at the deep end. I was introduced to the staff in the classroom and left to explain to them what I was doing there. The senior teacher and speech therapist introduced me to the children who were practising their parts in the forthcoming school play. Unfortunately, I could neither understand the words of the children who spoke to me nor communicate with those children who did not employ the spoken word as a means of communication. This resulted in me relying on the staff to explain what the children said or signed. I found my admission into the school a quite frightening experience. On a personal basis, I didn't have a clue how I was expected to behave by staff and children and I found it extremely difficult to understand if the children were happy with my presence in their class. This led to a lot of standing around, getting in the way of children and staff, until my role in the class developed. This uncomfortable experience was compounded by my academic related fear that I would be unable to fulfil the requirements of my post – to develop interactions with disabled children in order to understand their social worlds.
>
> (S1 – 15/5/97)

The outcome of this situation was that John was, at first, only able to tap into adult versions of the reality of life in the school. The most prominent message coming from the staff was contained in this comment:

> These children don't think like us, it's impossible to know what they are thinking. Our children have severe difficulties communicating and if our children's machines break down then, unlike us, they can't see the cause and effect. They don't understand why it has happened and that until it is fixed it won't work again. They have no concept of the continuum.
>
> (S1 – 15/5/97)

Some children were dependent on machines to communicate (e.g. speech board), others employed them to move round the school (e.g. power chair) or as a means of entertainment (e.g. power scooter). This teacher believed that the children did not understand how their machines worked and therefore, that they lacked certain cognitive abilities.

One of our aims, on entering the school, was to discuss issues of informed consent, confidentiality and so forth with the staff and children (Alderson

1995; Morrow and Richards 1996). John explained these issues to the staff. However, they appeared to reject the premise that the children would know what was going on. The adults whom John met seemed concerned that he understood that the children's impairments made them 'not like us'. The staff appeared to challenge John's idea that he should explain the research to the children, we as a team were reminded of Wax's (1971) comments, that people will often try to resocialize the researcher. It was clear that the staff were attempting to influence John's views and have him believe that these children were incapable of thinking for themselves.

John felt immense pressure to conform to their view. It was as if his permission to enter the research setting was granted on the grounds that he accept the staff's view that communication with these children would be troublesome due to their cognitive difficulties. These experiences revealed an immense gulf between the staff's view of the children and the research teams preconceptions that children should be treated as competent social actors and that understanding these children would be a task involving reflexivity and hermeneutical exchange.

At first John found himself differentiating between the children on the basis of their communication techniques, moreover he found himself spending more time with those children who could (verbally or through signs) answer yes and no to questions. He began to set up in his mind a hierarchy based on his perception of the abilities of the children. The process of gaining access to the school and learning to communicate with the children meant that he himself was attributing status to the children, he was judging them in terms of how easy they were to talk (verbally or non-verbally) to. John's constant exposure to the staff's negative views of the children eventually led him to question whether a number of the children in the class were capable of social interaction. However, a comment from Laura, a senior teacher, brought these perceptions into question:

> Like you wonder if someone like Jordan says a phrase that he's been taught or if he means it or if he is reproducing a set response, or Bobby he has his box with buttons to press for replies but if he's trying to tell you about home he may press the button for his address and rather than say 'I know where you live' you have to ask 'What is it about home?' The problem is that some of the less travelled staff don't look for the signs, they don't realise that the child is complaining about something or saying No. Like Scott when he shakes his fist they think he's being aggressive and he's not.
>
> (S1 – 20/8/97)

This account differentiates both between the children on the grounds of their cognitive and communication abilities which are identified with their impairment and between the staff on the grounds of their interpretation skills.

Although this comment reinforced some of John's ideas about the children, Laura's views concerning 'less travelled staff' suggested that how the adults interpreted the children's behaviour depended on their cultural background which related to their prior experience and preconceptions. It appeared that adults who were not reflexive about their interpretations missed the significance of the children's behaviour, and thus denied their ability to initiate meaningful communication. This lesson was crucial in the case of the relationship between the researcher and Scott, one of the boys at the school.

At first John had been unable to understand the meaning of his interactions with Scott and though we were interested in developing new research tools to aid the process of communication, in the end, we did not employ any pre-prepared 'child centred' or structured activities (Mauthner 1997). In keeping with James (1995), we recognized that the children we worked with had different competencies and experiences. In this setting this meant John was unable to employ techniques such as 'draw and write' (Pridmore and Bendelow 1995) or structured focus groups (Alderson 1995; Hoppe et al. 1995) or ask the children to make tape recordings (Mahon et al. 1996).

However, he was able to adapt to the everyday situations created by the structure of the school day. John began to get to know Scott, for example, by asking him questions about his home life during breaks. Scott responded to his questions by shaking his fist or nodding his head. John attended a signs and symbols class where he worked with Scott gluing pictures on to A4 paper to make a picture story and during this class Scott spoke about his family. John realized that Scott had chosen not to speak to him and that he had previously mistakenly interpreted Scott's behaviour as meaning Scott could not communicate. This realization came about because John attended the school on a daily basis which enabled him to interact with the children in a number of different educational settings.

This experience led us as a group to recall Agar's (1980) suggestion that when people withhold their opinion it does not necessarily mean they do not have an opinion. We decided that we should review John's first impressions of different children. Through analysing John's field notes it became apparent that John had allowed the staff's discourse to influence his perspective and therefore, to shape the manner in which he interacted with the children. He had failed to recognize the children's social ability to withhold access to their world; he had ignored the concept that children are the final gatekeepers to their worlds (Mandell 1991).

At the same time as we gained new understanding of the relevance of parts of John's field notes, our discussions enabled John to draw on experiences, his knowledge of the school setting, which had not been written down. That is, things that had previously been discounted or forgotten suddenly became relevant and new themes developed which required further investigation. Making mistakes, as Agar (1980) observes, can be fruitful in terms of creating opportunities for ethnographers to learn about the people they are studying. By realizing John's mistake, through a powerful fieldwork moment, we were able to develop new research questions: how had the different children reacted to him coming to their school? Could the staff be differentiated (as Laura had indicated) on the basis of how they attributed meaning to the same child's behaviour? Did all the staff share the same view of each child's capabilities?

These questions were stimulated by John's early experiences which forced us to question our perspectives of both children and staff. We recognized that at the same time as we were learning about the different lives of the children we had, at first, homogenized the behaviour of the adults who worked in the school. By analysing what staff said about specific children and the meanings that they attributed to children's behaviour, we were able to differentiate between the staff and build up a complex picture of the relationships between children and staff. Therefore, the very process of gaining access was employed as a research tool (Wax 1971) and the impact of the researcher on the research setting was analysed as a source of cultural meaning (Okely 1975). By analysing the effect of John's presence on the research setting, as recommended by Campbell (1995), we had discovered a great deal about his and our own cultural assumptions.

Indeed, our initial aim which was to study the experience of disabled children, taking seriously their role as social actors, negotiating their own social worlds, was broadened to include an understanding of how these negotiations were influenced by the variety of adults in the school. This process involved comparing the teachers' initial assertions that the children 'do not think like us' with the more nuanced view of Laura which differentiated between groups of staff and children.

This experience reminded us of Agar's (1980) advice that researchers should be aware that what respondents tell them at first may be a generalization of their beliefs which contrast with their actual behaviour and that it is usual, at times, for some informant's views to be incompatible with the interpretations of other informants and the ethnographer. In this case we realised that the children might not confer with what some of the teachers said about their lives but that to discover this John would have to learn how to interpret their language.

Learning Languages

We realized that the process of learning how to communicate with the children would take time and that as the ethnography unfolded this task would require the adoption of imaginative fieldwork roles and constant reflexivity. That John had to learn a number of unwritten, rarely verbal, languages could have been a galling task, however, we drew strength from Campbell's (1995) work with the Wayapi' people of the Brazilian rain forest. Campbell taught us that it is possible to learn an unwritten language:

No dictionaries, no grammars; and no training in how to go about this most mysterious of all learning procedures. I had no idea what I was up against, what to look for, whether it would even be possible to 'learn the language' at all. Could there be such a thing in the world as a language that was impossible to penetrate? No there isn't. The bafflement of Babel is accompanied by the miracle of translation. Wherever languages find each other, time and again the astonishing processes of translation begin to grow. It didn't come easy for me though.

(Campbell 1995: 34)

Campbell was aided in his task by Waiwai, the non-authoritarian head of the group he lived with. Whilst travelling, Waiwai taught Campbell the language:

Three days just ambling back the way the four of us had come. I'd walk behind Waiwai . . . Waiwai would cut leaf after leaf and get me to shout its name. I'd try to write as we walked along and try to think up some way of remembering what the leaf looked like. This was his way of teaching me the language: learn the words for all the leaves . . . As a botanical lesson it was hopeless for me, but it was as good a way into the language as any, getting a feel for the phonemes and the word structure.

(Campbell 1995: 21)

John's most helpful teacher was Rose the speech therapist. She taught him that most of the children understood his language and where they did not, for example children with hearing impairments, she taught him a form of sign language.[7] The main task, therefore, became to learn how the children communicated their responses. This process was easiest with children who used some speech and had similar interests to John. For example two boys Douglas and Bobby enjoyed football: discussions about different teams and various players enabled John to learn, very quickly, their way of communicating. In contrast, Lucy appeared not to employ recognizable signs. She had nipped John quite viciously on several occasions when he was sitting next to her. He thought this might be of significance until a teacher said that Lucy's behaviour was a reflex action. However, on a later occasion he was discussing Lucy with Rose and she said, 'The way into Lucy is to comment on her appearance, she takes that very seriously.' John realized that his gender had been affecting his interactions with the children: as a man he had guessed which subjects interested Bobby and Douglas, yet he had failed to identify what Lucy's interests might be.

Over the next few weeks John commented on Lucy's appearance, the way she looked each day, her make-up, nail varnish and clothing. Lucy never seemed to respond with a recognizable sign, yet she stopped nipping him.

John was encouraged by this change. Eventually, Lucy started responding to his questions with a grimace for no and a smile for yes. This enabled John to discover what food she wanted for lunch, which staff she liked and what activities she wanted to do when the staff gave the children options. In this way the social distance was reduced between them

When we discussed this as a team we realized that this confirmed the anthropological view that access to a culture is contingent on negotiating the meaning of everyday cultural artefacts – in this example nail polish/ clothing, in Campbell's example leaves. Central to this negotiation was John's role of 'fashion commentator' which changed the nature of John's interaction with Lucy. Thus, John adopted a number of research roles within the school which had complementary and contrasting meanings.

Research Roles

A number of authors have discussed the role an adult should employ when researching young people. Roles such as non-authoritarian adults (Mandell 1991; Fine 1987; Corsaro 1985), 'friends' (Fine and Sandstrom 1988), 'least adults' (Mandell 1991) and detached observers (Damon 1977) are recommended on the basis that they provide the researcher with the opportunity to interact with children.

All of these works arise from a concern to alter the power relations between adult and children in order that the researcher can gain access to children's worlds (Morrow and Richards 1996; Mayall 1994). They also support the notion, as we do, that researchers should empower children (Alderson 1995; Morrow and Richards 1996; Ross and Ross 1984), understanding their emotions (Levin 1994) and recognizing their fears (Beresford 1997).[8] It was our belief that if, as argued earlier, there were a number of different children's cultures present in the research setting then ethnographers not only may have to bridge the cultural gap between themselves (as adults) and the children but also have to understand the differences within and between different groups of children and different groups of adults.

As discussed, the process of gaining access to the research setting immediately illustrated differences within the adult and child groupings, differences which were made more explicit when a variety of adults and children invited John to carry out contrasting roles such as Friend/ Mediator/Entertainer and Authoritarian/Non-Authoritarian Adult/Helper.

Friend/Mediator/Entertainer Role

The staff encouraged John to take part in play activities such as ball throwing, card games of snap, dressing up, parachute games and relay races, which enabled him to adopt a playful friend role. However, it should be noted that this process often involved other adults and positioned John as playing for rather than with the children (for an elaboration of this issue see Priestley et al. 1999).

John developed a particularly fruitful relationship with a boy called Bobby. Bobby would respond to questions by saying 'aye' and 'no' and using signs. John learnt that Bobby employed various ways of saying 'no' and 'aye' which had different meanings. He also learnt that some staff had difficulty communicating with Bobby, that this led them to fail to comprehend the meaning of Bobby's actions and that, in some way, this was due to their tendency to undervalue (not attribute capital to) his behaviour (Bourdieu 1986). Over time Bobby began to ask John to translate his language for certain members of staff. However, in keeping with the advice of a number of children's researchers about the power relations involved in relationships with children (Morrow and Richards 1996; Mayall 1994), John would usually encourage Bobby to speak or sign for himself.[9] Towards the end of the project this role enabled John to understand how problems with the interpretative process led to conflict between Bobby and some members of staff (in this example, concerning the discussion of the result of a football match, the member of staff is Sharon):

John: [Bobby and I are crossing the room, Sharon an assistant and Rangers supporter starts speaking to us]

Sharon: Well John did you see the game last night? [Rangers had played Celtic the previous evening]

John: Aye, a wis there. Av almost lost ma voice shouting so much.

Sharon: Bobby did you watch the game last night?

Bobby: Aye.

Sharon: [looking at me as if to say, 'I don't believe him watch this I'll catch him out'] Who won then?

Bobby: [Puts his hands in the air and gets frustrated] uh, uh, uh, [like he's trying to spit something out but he just can't]

Sharon: See he doesn't know [said in a triumphal way to me, then whispers, even though Bobby still can hear her]. A don't think he really knows what's going on. A really don't think he understands.

John: [Bobby is really 'pissed off' with this and shakes his hands and head. I'm sure he watched the game because he spoke to me in signs earlier. Also I think he's finding it difficult to answer her question because the game was a draw and he can't say that word. He looks like he's going to give up, that he doesn't think he can make Sharon understand. I've had enough of Sharon so I decide to intervene.]

John: Na na I don't agree Sharon, a think he knows.

Bobby: Aye, aye.

Sharon: So what was the score? [still with disbelief]

John: Look a know that he doesn't usually watch the football but am sure he seen this game. Ay Bobby, now you tell me with signs, how many did Rangers score?

Bobby: [*Puts one finger up*]

John: [*Without confirming he's right*] and how many did we [*Celtic*] get?

Bobby: [*Puts up one finger*]

John: So the score was one one?

Bobby: Aye [*said with triumph and gestures at Sharon with his hand as if to say so there*]

John: And which team were lucky?

Bobby: [*Really laughing at the assistant because she's a Rangers supporter, he uses a word I've rarely heard him speak*] Isss [*us*].

Sharon: [*With a Damascus type conversion tone in her voice*] That's really good Bobby a nivir realised that.

(S1 – 25/11/97)

This incident demonstrates John's empowering role and the importance of closely attending to the children's ways of communicating. He creates the circumstances through which Bobby can empower himself. John employs his knowledge of Bobby's communication methods to ask questions structured in a form which Bobby preferred and could respond to. He helps Bobby to get his message across, a role which could potentially have brought John into conflict with Sharon. However, his reward for taking this chance was to make Bobby happy and it was his friendship role with Bobby which had forced him to question the legitimacy of Sharon's interpretation. In this way, John's relationship with Bobby contrasted with the authoritarian role which was expected of him by some staff and children in other situations.

Authoritarian/Non-Authoritarian Adult/Helper Role

Particularly in a school setting an additional adult is often expected to help with supervision and surveillance of the children. John was reluctant to play this role, which stemmed from our perspective that it might alienate him from some of the children. However, in contrast to the friendship role, some of the staff and children did expect John to adopt an authoritarian role. For example, John was placed in a very difficult position by the music teacher Margaret during a class which involved three boys called Scott, Douglas and Jordan:

John: [*Douglas, Jordan and Scott are in the music class. Scott is banging the drum when it's not his turn*]

Margaret: No! Scott! [*shouting*]

Douglas: That's not funny Scott.

Scott: [*Shakes his fist at Douglas in disagreement but also laughs*]

John: [*Scott continues to bang the drum when Margaret doesn't want him to*]

Margaret: [*To me*] Would you hold Scott's hand until it's his turn to do it?

John: [*I'm horrified. I don't just grab his hand*] Scott, shall I hold your hand? [*I put my hand out and he doesn't stop me holding his left hand*]

Margaret: [*Insistently*] No! The other hand.

John: I'm getting there, I rather thought I'd let Scott get used to me before putting the cuffs on.

Scott: [*Laughs and lets me lightly hold the hand with the beater*]

John: [*I decide not to hold his hand all class. I let his hand go, after which Scott only occasionally tries to hit the cymbal when it's not his turn. On these occasions I say, 'Is it your turn?' and he stops*]

Later Margaret talked to John about the boys:

Margaret: Jordan, sometimes you want to just give him a boot, Scott just won't behave but Douglas's good at picking the different sounds higher and lower, not that that's what I'm teaching.

(S1 – 3/9/97)

In this example, the teacher demands that John take an authoritarian role by controlling Scott's hands. John voices his concern and waits to see if Scott will consent to him holding his hands. His decision was based on our ethical perspective that children should be able to choose whether or not to interact with ethnographers. The teacher becomes very impatient with this approach and chastises John for not acting more quickly. Although John controls Scott's actions, Scott does not appear to mind. During this occurrence John's role changes from controller to that of coercer when he keeps saying 'Is it your turn?' That is, he stops controlling Scott's body and tries to encourage him to follow the teacher's rules. John is put in a very difficult situation. Refusing to help the teacher might compromise his position in the school with the staff, but carrying out her wishes might alienate him from Scott. His decision was to ask Scott's permission but it is difficult to know if, in doing so, he was really giving Scott a choice.

Interestingly in the above example, Douglas sided with the teacher and in a later music class he asked John to hold Jordan's hands when he was beating a drum out of time. This experience enabled John to differentiate between the children who conformed to the staff's wishes and those who did not. Moreover, it demonstrated that this member of staff, the music teacher, did not employ empowering techniques to encourage Scott to participate in the class.

We learned from these events that John, by paying close attention to the requests made of him by children and staff, could identify individual children's and adults' perceptions of him and therefore, contrast their every-day values and expectations with his own. This enabled us to roughly group the adults and children on the basis of how they interacted with John. Again, by discussing this occurrence in our weekly meeting, we were able to allow these events to guide the next stages of the research process. A number of questions were identified for John to follow up, for example, why did a specific child ask John to do the same things as other adults in a classroom setting? Did Scott recognize John as different from the music teacher or had this incident led to Scott viewing John as possessing an authoritarian role?

An opportunity arose to clarify this later question a week after the music class incident. Scott and a number of other boys had just finished their lunch. One boy, Jason, suggested that John put Bobby's splints on. John, realizing the situation, provided an opportunity to gain an insight on how the children viewed him, asked the children if they thought he should do this. Scott, through the use of signs, indicated that this was not John's role but the role of the occupational therapist, a teacher and an auxiliary who were all standing towards the far end of the room. Scott clearly did not associate John's role with that of other adults in the school. His view contrasted with the perception of Jason, who believed that John should put on Bobby's splints, and Douglas, who asked John to hold Steven's hands in the music class. This suggested to John that some children were happy to accept the authoritarian role of adults whereas others were not. Importantly, it exposed the myth that in this school these children could not make choices with regard to their everyday lives.

Our research aim, to be reflexive about John's research roles, required him and us to question why certain roles made him feel happy, uncomfortable, nervous and so on. This process was especially important in a research set-ting where there were a number of different adult and child expectations concerning the researcher's role. Indeed, John's experience was comparable to that of Mandell (1991), who was forced into a variable role which juggled the expectations of adults and children. John needed to be flexible and he was obliged to become aware that associating himself too closely with one cultural grouping might alienate himself from children and adults who possessed a different idea of what constituted acceptable behaviour. In keep-ing with the ideas of Wax (1971) and Agar (1980) the flexible negotiation of John's roles became a tool for understanding the cultures of those he inter-acted with.

In Bourdieu's (1986) terms John became acutely aware of how different social actors attributed cultural capital to different social practices, how they made judgements about their own and other people's behaviour. This led us to criticize Bearison's (1991) expectation that the researcher's role should be to represent children's voices but not to judge children's words. The ethnographic process involved John constantly making judgements and interpretations. What was important was that we questioned John's role in this process and that this inquisitorial stance also enabled us to understand the processes through which different children and adults judged each other's capabilities within the school.

John's variable role also enabled us to understand the structural influences surrounding the children, when John asked the staff or, when the staff offered, to explain the policy or aim which underpinned a specific role. By comparing how different adults carried out the same role, by experiencing the role himself and by noticing when there was a failure in procedure or when aims were not met, John learnt that everyday life in the school related to wider social factors. For example, the children came to this school from different local authority areas. Each of these authorities had its own policy and practice concerning when and how the children were 'dropped off' in the morning and 'picked up' from school in the afternoon. The school policy that each child should be toileted before leaving for home meant that the staff had to organize the children to go to the toilet prior to the end of the school day. This process meant the children were rarely given a choice about when they went to the toilet in the afternoon and how they governed their own bodily practice (see also Mayall 1994). Their bodily practice was inseparable from the social and cultural context of their lives (Bourdieu 1986).

Conclusion

As is evident from the examples given in this chapter, different adult cultures had, in contrasting ways, a structuring effect on the children's lives. The children in our study were well aware of the need to adapt their behaviour to certain adults and to the different settings of their everyday life at school in the manner suggested by Mayall (1994) and James and Prout (1995). They were aware (just as we researchers discovered) that adults can close off or open up opportunities for children to make their own choices. Sometimes they found opportunities themselves to negotiate their choices during interactions with adults. That is, in some way, they construct their own childhoods.

Thus, neither adults nor children are homogeneous groups, both actively create their own cultures within a set of pronounced cultural and structural constraints. Their lives involve a synthesis of structure, culture and agency which can be illustrated through ethnography. As Marcus (1986) has suggested, it is possible within a strategically selected single locale, such as a school, to combine 'accounts of impersonal systems into representations of local life as cultural forms both autonomous and constituted by the larger order' (Marcus 1986: 170). That is, to show how structural influences in society are often played out when people interact. This does not involve the construction of a specific childhood (see James et al. 1998) in terms of macro-social issues such as gender, social class, race and impairment. We have illustrated a process in which it is possible to differentiate between different groups of children on the basis of their everyday cultures. This has enabled us both to substantiate the suggestion that disabled children are not a homogeneous cultural grouping and to indicate that, like other children, disabled children are not 'simply passive subjects of structural determinations' (James and Prout 1990: 6).

In this chapter, therefore, we have highlighted the benefits of employing ethnographic fieldwork as a means of researching children. As James and Prout (1990) indicate, ethnography provides researchers with an opportunity to carry out participant observation with children which allows for detailed understandings of their everyday interactions and cultural meanings. As Davis (1998) argues, the ethnographic process results in the ethnographer being confronted by conflicting ethical issues on a daily basis and here we have described how these issues were negotiated with children and adults. The ethnographic process enables the ethnographer to learn about different children's cultures by analysing the ongoing and changing relationships children have with other people. At the same time, ethnographic research can, through the use of reflexivity, enable cultural meanings to be elucidated from the roles, tools and ethical stances employed by ethnographers during the research process. Thus, children's researchers can develop understandings of children's lives by utilizing the opportunities provided by the organizational structures and cultural artefacts to be found in children's social worlds, rather than structuring special and specific research opportunities. In this way, the use of ethnographic methods enabled us to challenge the perception that disabled children are not capable of social action and to argue that the social worlds of disabled children are as fluid as that of other social actors. By following Okely's (1975) assertion that ethnography does not involve a separation of fieldwork and analysis we were able to conclude that researchers who work within the social model of disability should not only aim to demonstrate the structural barriers which affect disabled people's lives but also aim to illustrate how the structural issues of disability are played out and created through social interaction between individuals and between groups. This leads us to conclude that when certain authors represent the structural and material aspects of childhood (see for example Qvortrup 1994 and Chapter 4 in this volume), they should be asked to explain how these factors are negotiated and (in the case of social policies) implemented by different individuals and groups (whether they be children or adults) on a daily basis.

J. Davis, N. Watson, S. Cunningham-Burley

Acknowledgements

Many thanks to Mairian Corker, Pia Christensen and Allison James for their comments on earlier drafts of this chapter. This chapter draws on our current experiences of working on a project which is part of the ESRC research programme, Children 5–16: Growing into the 21st Century. Our project aims to gain an insight into what it means to be a young disabled person, aged 11–16, through investigating their own perspectives.

Notes

1 We do not intend to provide any further information on the nature of the school in order to avoid the possibility that the identity of the school and, therefore, our respondents are recognized.
2 We are carrying out ethnographic research which involves participant observation in a number of settings – special and mainstream schools, play schemes and clubs, homes and neighbourhoods. The aim of this approach is to include young people as active participants, so that they can contribute to shaping the direction, content and techniques we employ throughout the research process. The project is being carried out at the universities of Edinburgh and Leeds.
3 Elsewhere this has been related to the shifting roles employed while researching children (Davis 1998; Corker and Davis 1999).
4 See Corker and Davis (1999) for an explanation of how reflexivity is employed by two ethnographers (one deaf, one hearing) researching the same setting.
5 It should be noted that these preconceptions in some part stemmed from the usual academic process of carrying out a literature prior to carrying out research.
6 Interestingly, we do not believe this group of authors' illustration of different childhoods to be the same as the sociological abstractions outlined within certain texts (e.g. the labels such as 'tribal child' and 'social structural child' created by James et al. 1998). That is, we perceive the first types of childhoods to be grounded in data concerning children's lived experiences and we would argue that the later discussion of childhoods are concerned with abstractions grounded in certain authors' sociological imaginations. We believe that children are capable of developing multiple identities which they draw from when operating in different fields (James and Prout 1995; Connelly 1998). Indeed, we are concerned that this perspective may be downplayed as an unintended consequence of the use of such labels.
7 This learning process was helped by the fact that the whole team were, at that time, learning British Sign Language at night school.
8 It should be noted that our idea of empowerment, in keeping with writers concerned with the social model of disability discussed in this chapter, is grounded in the belief that people (child or adult) empower themselves and that our role should be to avoid erecting barriers which might block this process.
9 Morrow and Richards (1996) have argued that the power of adults can be reduced by employing techniques which enabled children to become part of the research process. See Davis (1998) for an explanation of our perspective with regard to the ethics, roles and tools employed by children's researchers.

References

Abberley, P. (1987) 'The concept of oppression and the development of a social theory of disability', *Disability, Handicap and Society* 2(1): 5–19.

Agar, M.H. (1980) *The Professional Stranger*, New York: Academic Press.

Alan, J. (1996) 'Foucault and special educational needs: a "box of tools" for analysing children's experience of mainstreaming', *Disability and Society* 11(2): 219–33.

Alderson, P. (1993) *Children's Consent to Surgery*, Buckingham: Open University Press.

Alderson, P. (1995) *Listening to Children: Children, Ethics and Social Research*, Barkingside: Barnardo's.

Alderson, P. and Goodey, C. (1998) 'Doctors, ethics and special education', *Journal of Medical Ethics* 24(1): 49–55.

Aldersons, P. and Goodey, C. (1998) *Enabling Education: Experiences in Special and Ordinary Schools*, London: Tufnell Press.

Barnes, C. (1991) *Disabled People in Britain and Discrimination: A Case for Anti-Discrimination Legislation*, London: Hurst.

Bearison, D.J. (1991) *They Never Want to Tell You: Children Talk about Cancer*, Cambridge, MA: Harvard University Press.

Beresford, B. (1997) *Personal Accounts: Involving Disabled Children in Research*, Norwich: Social Policy Research Unit.

Bourdieu, P. (1986) *Distinction*, London: Routledge.

Brannen, J. and O Brian, M. (1995) 'Childhood and the sociological gaze: paradigms and paradoxes', *Sociology* 29(4): 729–37.

Callaway, H. (1992) 'Ethnography and experience: gender implications in fieldwork and texts', in J. Okely and H. Callaway (eds) *Anthropology and Autobiography*, London: Routledge.

Campbell, A.T. (1995) *Getting to Know Waiwai: An Amazonian Ethnography*, London: Routledge.

Connolly, P. (1998) *Racism, Gender Identities and Young Children*, London: Routledge.

Corker, M. and Davis, J.M. (1999) 'Shifting selves, shifting meanings, learning culture – deaf and hearing researchers working with disabled children', Paper to Deaf Education Studies Seminar, University of Birmingham, October 1998.

Corsaro, W. (1985) *Friendship and Peer Culture in the Early Years*, Norwood, NJ: Ablex.

Crapanzano, V. (1986) 'Hermes' dilemma: the masking of subversion in ethnographic description', in J. Clifford and G.E. Marcus (eds) *Writing Culture: The Poetics and Politics of Ethnography*, Berkeley: University of California Press.

Damon, W. (1977) *The Social World of the Child*, San Francisco, CA: Jossey-Bass.

Davis, J.M. (1996) 'Sport for all?', Ph.D. thesis, University of Edinburgh.

Davis, J.M. (1998) 'Understanding the meanings of children: a reflexive process', *Children and Society* 12(5): 325–36.

Davis, J.M. (1999) *Culture, Structure and Agency in Lothian PE Settings*, 1998–99 Scottish Centre Research Papers in Sport, Leisure and Society 3: 1–14, Edinburgh: Scottish Centre for Physical Education Sport.

Fine, G.A. (1987) *With the Boys*, Chicago: University of Chicago Press.

Fine, G.A. and Sandstrom, K.L. (1988) *Knowing Children: Participant Observation with Minors*, Newbury Park, CA: Sage.

Finkelstein, V. (1975) 'To deny or not to deny disability', *Magic Carpet* 28(1): 31–8.

Geertz, C. (1973) *The Interpretation of Cultures*, New York: Basic Books.

Giddens, A. (1976) *New Rules of Sociological Methods*, London: Hutchinson.

Glauser, B. (1990) 'Street children: deconstructing a construction', in A. James and A. Prout (eds) *Constructing and Reconstructing Childhood*, London: Falmer Press.

Hallden, G. (1994) 'The family – a refuge from demands or an arena for the exercise of power and control – children's fictions on their future families', in B. Mayall (ed.) *Children's Childhoods Observed and Experienced*, London: Falmer Press.

Hammersley, M. (1990) *Classroom Ethnography*, Milton Keynes: Open University Press.

Hammersley, M. and Atkinson, P. (1983) *Ethnography: Principles in Practice*, London: Routledge.

Hardman, C. (1973) 'Can there be an anthropology of children?', *Journal of the Anthropology Society of Oxford* 4: 85.

Hendry, L.B., Shucksmith, J., Love, J. and Glendenning, A. (1993) *Young People's Leisure and Lifestyles*, London: Routledge.

Hertz, R. (1997) 'Introduction', to Hertz (ed.) *Reflexivity and Voice*, London: Sage.

Hoppe, M.J., Wells, E., Morrison, D., Gilmore, M. and Wilson, A. (1995) 'Using focus groups to discuss sensitive topics with children', *Evaluation Review* 19: 102–14.

Humphries, S. and Gordon, P. (1992) *Out of Sight: The Experience of Disability 1900–1950*, Plymouth: Northcote House.

James, A. (1995) 'Methodologies of competence for competent methodology?', Paper to Youth 2000 Conference, Guildford, July.

James, A. and Prout, A. (1990) 'Contemporary issues in the sociological study of childhood', in A. James and A. Prout (eds) *Constructing and Reconstructing Childhood*. London: Falmer Press.

James, A. and Prout, A. (1995) 'Hierarchy, boundary and agency', *Sociological Studies in Children* 7: 77–99.

James, A., Jenks, C. and Prout, A. (1998) *Theorising Childhood*, Cambridge: Polity.

Levin, I. (1994) 'Children's perceptions of their families', in J. Brannen and M. O'Brien (eds) *Childhood and Parenthood: Proceedings of the International Sociological Association Committee for Family Research Conference*, London: Institute of Education, University of London.

Lewis, A. (1995) *Children's Understandings of Disability*, London: Routledge.

Mackay, R.W. (1991) 'Conceptions of children and models of socialisation', in F.C. Waksler (ed.) *Studying the Social Worlds of Children: Sociological Readings*, London: Falmer Press.

Mahon, A., Glendenning, C., Clarke, K. and Craig, G. (1996) 'Researching children: methods and ethics', *Children and Society* 10: 145–54.

Mandell, N. (1991) 'The least-adult role in studying children', in F.C. Waksler (ed.) *Studying the Social Worlds of Children: Sociological Readings*, London: Falmer Press.

Marcus, G. (1986) 'Contemporary problems of ethnography in the modern world system', in J. Clifford and G.E. Marcus (eds) *Writing Culture: The Poetics and Politics of Ethnography*, Berkeley, CA: University of California Press.

Marcus, G.E. and Fischer, M.J. (1986) *Anthropology as Cultural Critique*, Chicago: University of Chicago Press.

Mauthner, M. (1997) 'Methodological aspects of collecting data from children', *Children and Society* 11: 16–28.

Mayall, B. (1994) 'Children in action at home and school', in B. Mayall (ed.) *Children's Childhoods Observed and Experienced*, London: Falmer Press.

Middleton, L. (1996) *Making a Difference: Social Work with Disabled Children*, Birmingham: Venture Press.

Morris, J. (1991) *Pride Against Prejudice: Transforming Attitudes to Disability*, London: Women's Press.

Morris, J. (1997) 'Gone missing? Disabled children living away from their families', *Disability and Society* 12(2): 241–58.

Morrow, V. and Richards, M. (1996) 'The ethics of social research with children: an over view', *Children and Society* 10: 28–40.

Norwich, B. (1997) 'Exploring the perspectives of adolescents with moderate learning difficulties on their special schooling and themselves: stigma and self-perceptions', *European Journal of Special Needs Education* 12(1): 38–53.

Okely, J. (1975) 'The self and scientism', *Journal of the Anthropology Society of Oxford* 6: 171.

Okely, J. (1992) 'Anthropology and autobiography: participatory experience and embodied knowledge', in J. Okely and H. Callaway (eds) *Anthropology and Autobiography*, London: Routledge.

Okely, J. (1994) 'Thinking through fieldwork', in A. Bryman and R.G. Burgess (eds) *Analysing Qualitative Data*, London: Routledge.

Oliver, M. (1990) *The Politics of Disablement*, London: Macmillan.

Opie, I. and Opie, P. (1969) *Children's Gangs in Street and Playground,* Oxford: Oxford University Press.

Opie, I. and Opie, P. (1991) 'The culture of children', in F.C. Waksler (ed.) *Studying the Social Worlds of Children: Sociological Readings*, London: Falmer Press.

Prat, M. (1986) 'Fieldwork in common places', in J. Clifford and G.E. Marcus (eds) *Writing Culture: The Poetics and Politics of Ethnography*, Berkeley, CA: University of California Press.

Pridmore, P. and Bendelow, G. (1995) 'Images of health: exploring beliefs of children using the "draw-and-write technique"', *Health Education Journal* 54: 473–88.

Priestley, M. (1998) 'Childhood disability and disabled childhoods: agendas for research', *Childhood* 5(2): 207–23.

Priestley, M., Davis, J. and Watson, N. (1999) 'Play away: disabled children and anti-social spaces', *Urban Geography.*

Qvortrup, J. (1994) 'Childhood matters: an introduction', in J. Qvortrup et al. (eds) *Childhood Matters: Social Theory, Politics and Practice*, Aldershot: Avebury.

Ritala-Koskinen, A. (1994) 'Children and the construction of close relationships: how to find out the children's point of view', in J. Brannen and M. O'Brien

J. Davis, N. Watson, S. Cunningham-Burley

(eds) *Childhood and Parenthood*, London: Institute of Education, University of London.

Ross, D. and Ross, S. (1984) 'The importance of the type of question', *Pain* 19: 71–9.

Shakespeare, T. and Watson, N. (1998) 'Theoretical perspectives on research with disabled children', in C. Robinson and K. Stalker (eds) *Growing Up with Disability*, London: Jessica Kingsley.

Tammivaara, J. and Enright, S. (1986) 'On eliciting information: dialogues with child informants', *Anthropology and Education Quarterly* 17: 218–38.

Thomas, D. (1978) *The Social Psychology of Childhood Disability*, London: Methuen.

Thorne, B. (1993) *Gender Play: Girls and Boys in Schools*, New Brunswick, NJ: Rutgers University Press.

Tomlinson, S. and Colquhoun, R. (1995) 'The political economy of special educational needs in Britain', *Disability and Society* 10(2): 191–202.

UPAIS/Disability Alliance (1976) *Fundamental Principles of Disability*, London: Methuen.

Wartofsky, M. (1983) 'The child's construction of the world and the world's construction of the child', in F.S. Kessel and A. Siegel (eds) *The Child and Other Cultural Inventions*, New York: Praeger.

Wax, R.H. (1971) *Doing Fieldwork: Warnings and Advice*, Chicago: University of Chicago Press.

Zarb, G. (ed.) (1995) *Removing Disabling Barriers*, London: Policy Studies Institute.

11 Listening to Children: and Hearing Them

Helen Roberts

Introduction

In 1875, Andrew Doyle reported to the local government board at Whitehall on the emigration of pauper children to Canada. He spoke to many children, some of whom had happy experiences, some not. 'We all sicked over each other,' was one description of the sea voyage, while a child patiently explained: ''Doption sir, is when folks gets a girl to work without wages' (Doyle 1875) Thus, listening to children has a longer history than those of us currently interviewing children are inclined to acknowledge. Moreover, we are still not good enough at hearing them, in the sense of taking full account of what they tell us. As researchers, we are still learning ways of involving children fully in every stage of the research process from identifying meaningful research questions, to collaborating with researchers, and disseminating good practice. And we are still learning that there may be occasions when such involvement may itself be exploitative or inappropriate, just as in other cases, not to involve children and young people represents poor practice.

Increasingly local authorities and voluntary organizations are looking at ways of consulting children and young people, though it remains to be seen whether their voices will be heard. Moreover, children are an important consumer group, and as such, of growing interest to market researchers. A number of market research organizations have panels of children whom they can access, run school based surveys, and are adept at running children's focus groups. It is not only researchers with an interest in childhood who have an interest in children. The media, business people, politicians and policy-makers all have an interest in the views, the voice or the perspective of the child.

This should, of course, be good news in principle for those concerned with listening to children and enabling them to speak out. But given this burgeoning interest in children, what is there to stop children becoming merely a tool in the adult armoury, with no opportunity for genuine participation? Our awareness that there is not one set of views, one 'voice' or one perspective can be even more problematic when working with a powerless group, such as those children who are socially excluded, and in greatest need, than when researching or working with adults.

Child Research in Theory and Practice

The majority of contributions to this book are from scholars. The perspective from which I am writing this chapter is that of the R&D coordinator of the UK's largest childcare organization, Barnardo's (although the views expressed here are personal ones, and do not necessarily reflect Barnardo's policy). Founded in the late nineteenth century by Dr Thomas Barnardo, the charity has always worked with the issues facing children and young people in greatest need. While our approach has changed from one of child rescue to one which attempts to enable children and young people to thrive in their families and their communities, the issues with which we work are similar to those facing Dr Barnardo and his colleagues. Children and young people on the streets, children facing poverty, children disadvantaged through racism or disability are those with whom we worked then, and work now. We currently provide services to some 43,000 children and young people throughout the UK from over 285 project bases.

Research and development in Barnardo's is based in the Policy Planning and Research Unit of the organization, with R&D staff working closely with policy and practice, parliamentary and information science colleagues. The work of our section involves providing a resource for the evaluation of our practice, looking at the best available evidence of 'what works' for children experiencing difficulties and working to transfer this into practice, and providing an R&D service for the organization which treats children and young people as a reservoir of expertise on their own lives, and provides opportunities to consult with them in a meaningful way.

The ESRC research programme, Children 5–16: Growing into the 21st Century and initiatives from the Joseph Rowntree Foundation and the Carnegie Trust, among others, have ensured a welcome place for children, or for those who research them, in the research enterprise. The contribution of recent scholarship to our understanding of children's lives is crucial for those of us whose work is in policy and practice. One of Barnardo's charitable objects is to influence social welfare policy as it affects children and, in this, there are occasions when we can use the knowledge generated by scholars and others in lobbying, campaigning, or in negotiations with the local or national bodies.

However, research reports are only one of our sources. A real strength for all those of us who deliver services is that our work can draw not only on sound secondary data, but on the experiences of those with whom we work. For example, although the question of what counts as poverty may be contested in academic and political debates, the experience of a child living in poverty, vividly described, cannot so easily be dismissed. To generate sound work specifically aimed to serve to advocate the needs of children, our relationships with those on the receiving end of services are crucial. Water metering (McNeish 1993), school exclusions (Cohen et al. 1994) and the numbers of children and young people affected by their parent's HIV status for example (Imrie and Coombes 1995) were all identified through service users and practitioners well before they became big issues, and gave us as an organization the chance to have some influence in setting the agenda as well as responding to it. The ways in which an organization like Barnardo's can advocate for the needs of children, young people and their families will range from quiet diplomacy to more robust campaigning and lobbying at central or local level. Good advocacy depends crucially on a clear and detailed understanding of the situation on the ground. Our Streets and Lanes (SALS) project in Bradford, for example, works with young women under the age of consent who are sexually exploited (sometimes referred to as child prostitutes – but how can a girl who is too young to legally consent to sex be classed as a criminal and a prostitute?). Work initiated from the SALS project has resulted in a series of recommendations to the Home Office and the Department of Health, constructive meetings with the Association of Chief Police Officers and the Magistrates Association among others (Barnardo's 1998). Barnardo's is clear that the full force of existing legislation should be targeted at adults who abuse and exploit children. Meanwhile, with financial backing from the Department of Health's Section 64 funding earmarked for child protection services, schemes are being set up in various areas to provide direct services, to work with a police pilot in Wolverhampton set up to prosecute the men who abuse, rather than the girls involved, and to make contact with missing young women in Yorkshire.

Sometimes, Barnardo's will work as a single agency in its advocacy work, sometimes, in conjunction with other agencies such as other children's charities, or, in the case of water metering, the British Medical Association. It is important that the R&D underlying this advocacy is robust (certainly robust enough to withstand a grilling on the early morning *Today* BBC radio programme), and the combination of practice, research, policy and our charitable objects make it both appropriate and possible for us to be involved in advocacy in a way which might be less appropriate for scholarly researchers. The key issue is whether we are working in the interests of those we are set up to serve – children.

British industry, it is claimed, spends too much on dividends, and too little on R&D and investment. If this is so in industry (or the 'real world', as we in the parallel 'unreal' universe are urged to call it) how are we doing in child welfare? Are children in need getting sufficient dividends from our work? And how can we ensure that R&D works in their interests?

The following examples demonstrate some of the problems and dilemmas of listening to children, and the way in which it may be (or be perceived as) intrusive or inappropriate. While taking account of the views and feelings of children is one thing, parading them is quite another. Young children (and indeed many adults) may not always have the judgement to know what the consequences will be of exposing their feelings on television for instance.

A *Panorama* programme raised the issue of the distress children may feel during or after divorce. A tearful boy is televised during a therapy session. In the *Radio Times*, a viewer writes: 'Little [x] was clearly too young to have consented to the filming . . . The sequence was not necessary to establish the facts, simply public voyeurism of a small child's emotional exposure.' The editor replies, 'We took every care to portray [his] therapy session sensitively. Filming took place with the consent of both parents and the therapists . . . [Name] himself was keen to tell his story.'

Within social research too, there are examples of children participating in research where they may well suffer distress (Grodin and Glantz 1994). One example from psychological research is the classic 'fear of strangers' experiment, where young babies are briefly separated from their mothers, and their response to the entry of a stranger and their mother's return are used as a test for the strength and quality of their emotional attachment (see Woodhead and Faulkner, Chapter 1). The babies' distress is usually short-lived, but often quite intense. What or whom does this experiment serve? Do we learn anything from it, and if we do, is it worthwhile?

Nor is the history of social care without examples of children harmed by interventions intended for their good; the denial of information about their family of origin to adopted children was a case in point. It was frequently felt that children needed a fresh start in a new family, and that contact with the past would be counter-productive. There now appears to be good evidence that maintaining a link with the past is in many cases very positive (Sellick and Thoburn 1996.) Children in institutional care have been particularly prone to well-meaning experimentation (though we are loath to call it that) in which their voices, even if listened to, go unheard. The Doyle report (1875), referred to at the start of this chapter, is a case in point. It was not until the 1960s that the programmes sending children overseas from the UK terminated. Moreover, we know from the litany of inquiries into child abuse in residential care that in many cases, children had signalled their distress but this had not been taken sufficiently seriously. This enabled brutality to continue, and half-baked theories to flourish unchallenged.

This chapter explores the possibilities and problems of listening to children from the perspective of a researcher in a large voluntary childcare organization. It describes three specific initiatives carried out within Barnardo's, aimed at listening to children with a view to affecting policy and practice.

Listening to Children: Children, Ethics and Social Research

Since research questions and research agendas are still largely the province of adults, children's narratives tend to be edited, reformulated or truncated to fit our agendas in much the same way as Graham (1983, 1984) elegantly describes in her account of the way in which women's lives are poorly served by some of social science's traditional research methods. Graham suggests that the narrative tradition is one way of solving the problem of the fracturing of experiences which may occur through traditional research methods such as questionnaires and surveys.

Similarly, listening to children is central to recognizing and respecting their worth as human beings. Children are not simply objects, either of concern, of research or of a media story. But while in medicine, ethics committees may offer some (albeit imperfect) protection, no such formal ethical procedures exist for children and young people asked to take part in social interventions, or social research. For this reason, Barnardo's commissioned work which would enable us to consider, and share with others in the child welfare community, ethical issues arising from research with children, including an element part-funded by the Calouste Gulbenkian Foundation on the training of young interviewers (Alderson 1995). We were aware then, as we continue to be, that researching children and trying to involve children and young people in decisions touching on their lives does not necessarily place researchers or others on the high moral ground, above those who in the bad old days would research children or intervene in their lives without so much as a focus group or questionnaire. It cannot be taken for granted that more listening means more hearing, or that the cost benefits to children of participating in research on questions in which they may or may not have a stake is worth the candle.

Thus although ethical guidelines do not give us the answers, they can lead us to ask the right kinds of questions. Alderson (1995) in her work for Barnardo's suggests ten topics that social researchers should address:

1 **The purpose of the research**: If the research findings are meant to benefit certain children, who are they, and how might they benefit?
2 **Researching with children – costs and hoped for benefits**: Might there be risks or costs such as time, inconvenience, embarrassment, intrusion of privacy, sense of failure or coercion, fear of admitting anxiety?
3 **Privacy and confidentiality**: When significant extracts from interviews are quoted in reports, should reseachers first check the quotation and commentary with the child (or parent) concerned?

4 **Selection, inclusion and exclusion**: Have some children been excluded because, for instance, they have speech or learning difficulties? Can the exclusion be justified?

5 **Funding**: Should the research funds be raised only from agencies which avoid activities that can harm children?

6 **Review and revision of the research aims and methods**: Have children or their carers helped to plan or commented on the research?

7 **Information for children, parents and other carers**: Are the children and adults concerned given details about the purpose and nature of the research, the methods and timing, and the possible benefits, harms and outcomes?

8 **Consent**: Do children know that if they refuse or withdraw from the research, this will not be held against them in any way? How do the researchers help children to know these things?

9 **Dissemination**: Will the children and adults involved be sent short reports of the main findings?

10 **Impact on children**: Besides the effects of the research on the children involved, how might the conclusions affect larger groups of children?

In addition to these guidelines, Alderson (1995) suggests as good practice, and provides an example of this, the production of explanatory leaflets for children and young people involved in research, helping them to understand what a project is about, ask the salient questions, and become part of the process rather than simply its objects of study.

What have the consequences of this work been within and beyond Barnardo's? It is frequently the case in scholarly life that the work of researchers, even the best researchers, languishes in journals with small readerships, or is presented at academic conferences but only peripherally touches the policy and practice domains. This is sometimes for the very good reason that the work is not intended for immediate 'use'. It may, for instance, be highly theoretical, and in that sense, academic in the best sense of the term. Sometimes, though, scholars intend their work to be used, and are baffled, hurt or unpleasantly surprised when, even after efforts to influence users, their work is not taken up. This will frequently be because 'user organizations' have their own knowledge, agendas, cadences and timetables. They are more likely to be influenced by a piece of research if they have been involved from the planning stage onwards. Alderson's work provides an example of ways in which academics and user groups, such as Barnardo's, can work well together. It was commissioned by a user organization on the basis of a fairly tight specification of what we perceived as gaps in the ways in which both child welfare organizations and the academy approached research with children. Dissemination plans were made from the outset. At Barnardo's we were clear who we wanted to influence and why, and what the avenues open to us might be. Our first step, as is the case with the majority of the work we commission, was to set up an advisory group. These groups vary from one project to another, but this particular project advisory group comprised policy, research and practice perspectives from our own organization, as well as our parliamentary officer, a representative from a government department, a senior journalist who writes on children's issues, and a number of researchers from other academic and children's sector organizations. The director of the (then) Children's Rights Development Unit (now the Children's Rights Office) was also an active member.

While Barnardo's takes the views of advisory groups, referees and other experts seriously, we are always clear that they are advisory (rather than, for instance, steering groups). Thus, the ultimate responsibility for the work and its successful dissemination rests with the research manager within our own organization who has responsibility for the project, working in tandem with the researcher and members of our press and publicity team.

This project was carried out to a tight timetable, with a dissemination conference planned for the launch, to which practitioners, researchers, market researchers and representatives from the Department of Health were invited. The conference itself was a sell out (only a proxy measure of success, to be sure, but a good early sign).

The immediate feedback, including from colleagues in the Department of Health, was very positive. But for those of us who work on the effectiveness of interventions, the acid test was whether it would have a wider influence, and more importantly, be used. In this sense, *Listening to Children: Children, Ethics and Social Research* (Alderson 1995) was an output, not an outcome. What might the longer term results be? Would a single child be better off as a result?

From this point of view, we were heartened to find that the publication was widely cited in applications to the ESRC Children 5–16 initiative and was influential in the genesis of two publications from the Joseph Rowntree Foundation, one on working with disabled children (Ward 1997) and the other on working with children and young people in groups (Hurley 1998). Again, in terms of a direct result for children, this can be only a proxy for success, but the development of guidelines suggesting respectful and inclusive ways of involving children in the research process is a step forward.

Everybody In? Involving Young People in the Research Process

A consequence of the work described above was the inclusion of some of the young people with whom we work in the development and conduct of a piece of research which Barnardo's was about to begin (see Alderson, Chapter 12). This resulted in a study conducted and co-authored by two of our professional researchers in collaboration with three young disabled men, involved in research for the first time (Ash et al. 1997a, 1997b). Lee Richardson, Marc Davies and Julian Bellew had been pupils at Barnardo's Princess Margaret

Helen Roberts

School in the west of England, and were recruited to help us carry out a piece of work designed to explore the views of disabled and non-disabled students on inclusive policies in further education. Their personal experience of separate education brought an invaluable perspective to the study. After training and discussion, they not only conducted first rate interviews with both able-bodied and disabled students, but also, in much the same way as Oakley (1981) had found in her study of motherhood, they faced questions from their interviewees. As Oakley (1981: 58) points out: 'personal involvement is more than dangerous bias – it is the condition under which people come to know each other and to admit others into their lives.' Just as Oakley was asked by her respondents whether it hurt to have a baby, and whether an epidural ever paralysed women, the limited opportunity which many young people have to discuss the experience of being disabled was illustrated by questions to our researchers such as: 'Have you two [researchers] ever felt that you've been prevented from doing things that you'd like to have a go at?' The interviewers, like Oakley, eschewed the traditional research manual approach, which suggests that the interviewer parries, avoids or otherwise discourages questions:

> Never provide the interviewee with any formal indication of the interviewer's beliefs and values.
>
> (Sjoberg and Nett 1968: 212)

> If he [the interviewer] should be asked for his views, he should laugh off the request with the remark that his job at the moment is to get opinions, not to have them.
>
> (Selltiz et al. 1965: 576)

Our colleagues chose to answer: 'Yes, I think a parent with a disabled child is far more protective' and

> Yes . . . In fact it makes me want to go ahead even stronger, and do it because you're being held back and held back. You go to special school, and at the time, we both actually loved it, but now I regret it so much because it's so wrong. You should all be able to go to the same school, to be with local people of the same background. I didn't know anyone where I lived – it's so wrong. It's even harder when you've got communication problems. It's such a barrier, people talk for you, and you don't get a chance to say anything. You're told you will do this, or you will do that, you know 'you will have a cup of tea,' or whatever.

Each response led to a new question:

How do you get round that problem then, of people making decisions for you?

Be a bit pig ignorant really. A bit rude sometimes.

This might sound like a stupid question, but do you feel that you fit in with everyone else now, or do you still feel that you're separate?

It depends really. You've really got to go out and compete. If you sit back in a corner then people won't talk to you. They'll just see you as an object. You've got to show that you can compete. It's not what you can't do. It's what you can do.

Our young interviewers, in this case, felt that it was right to share something of their lives with those they were researching. While it is unlikely that they would see their responses in terms of an educational intervention, it seems all too likely that the young people being interviewed were given a rare chance to learn something about the experience of disabled young people, and the disabling consequences of impairment. The questions, the methods and the composition of the research team serve to illustrate the importance of turning an abstract commitment to inclusion into something meaningful in day to day R&D practice as well as service delivery, an experience which has encouraged Barnardo's to do further work on the training of young interviewers, and experimenting with different forms of involvement of children and young people.

Young People's Social Attitudes

A further piece of work (discussed below) involves a large survey of social attitudes. When the first volume in Social and Community Planning Research's British Social Attitudes series was published (Jowell and Airey 1984), Sir Claus Moser, former head of the Government Statistical Service, welcomed an initiative which would enable civil servants, academics, journalists and others to explore how we think and feel as a nation. That first survey, and those which have followed, have tracked social attitudes via representative samples of adults living in Great Britain, and have provided one means by which we can begin to understand the way our beliefs, attitudes and values change over time. From the start, the survey has tracked the views of adults aged 18 or over. But what do we know of the attitudes of younger adults and children?

In 1993, Barnardo's approached Social and Community Planning Research (SCPR) with a proposal for a 'daughter' survey, based on young people in the households of adult respondents, to explore the social attitudes of a group of children and young people, which would be comparable to the adult survey in terms of both quality, and substantive subject matter. We have lacked the foundations for a regular, authoritative survey of the views and attitudes of young people, demonstrating the direction of any changes in social attitudes among young people. We know quite a lot about what adults think of young people and how that has changed over time. But how do they think we adults are doing? What are their views of right and wrong? What basic political knowledge do they have? What are their views on education, on the relationship between different ethnic groups or on gender inequalities? As others have pointed out, if we want to know about what people think of their world and themselves, there is no substitute for asking them (Turner and Martin 1981).

Barnardo's interest in this stemmed from our commitment to listening to young people and speaking out on their behalf or enabling them to speak out themselves. Barnardo's works with those in greatest need, but in order to understand the lives and values of those at the margins of society, we need to have access to the wider picture. The 'youth question' is a source of imagery of a turbulent character, and youthful deviance has been seen as a portent of intergenerational conflict. This conception coexists with less publicized studies, indicating mass adolescent conformity to core values and beliefs (Downes and Rock 1990). The Barnardo's/SCPR survey which resulted in the publication *Young People's Social Attitudes* (YPSA: Roberts and Sachdev 1996) provided an opportunity to look over time at these core attitudes and beliefs, and to compare these to the attitudes and beliefs of adults surveyed in British Social Attitudes (BSA: see also Brook 1996).

The YPSA questions were subject to piloting, and we had helpful feedback from the interviewers involved. It was useful both in that it provided reassurance on the issue of whether young people would be willing, able or interested in taking part in the work, and positive feedback from a group of interviewers who normally interviewed other adults. 'It's the easiest pilot I've done – they wanted to take part', 'It's good that children are being asked' and 'I couldn't believe the way they responded. It was brilliant.' One series of questions on the age at which children and young people should be expected to carry out household tasks such as washing up, or making their own beds resulted in some interesting comments. Interviewers discerned from the pilots a tendency of children to give an age one year older than they actually were. Other responses included (for washing up) 'when you can reach the sink'. One interviewer reported a child saying that the age at which children should be expected to help with these tasks was 'when I grow up'. The interviewer said 'I gave her a look to see if she was taking the mick, and she said, "No, I mean it. I'm a child. I'm going to have to do it for the rest of my life".'

The feedback from the pilot made it clear not only that children and young people could answer the questions, but also that they enjoyed being asked their opinions. Our findings did not present a picture of disaffected and rebellious youth. While the notion that 'young people like things pretty much the way that they are' would be unlikely to produce a successful newspaper headline (Newman 1996), the overall picture of young people portrayed by these data did not suggest that children and young people are storming the bastions of adult power. They wanted parents to have a bigger say than them in the educational curriculum, they felt that drug use at school should be punished, they did not believe that people should get married while very young, or leave school too early, and almost a third support current film censorship laws. At the same time, they expressed strong opinions on racial prejudice, crime prevention, justice and poverty. Young people were clearer about what they thought of God and religion than what they thought about politics. While a quarter of young people replied that they did not know how they would vote if a general election were held tomorrow, they were more decisive on 'belonging' to a religion, or belief in God.

No survey finding, of course, can be taken as a precise statement about young people's social attitudes in Britain. As Jowell (1984: 7) writes: 'Every finding is an approximation, part of a body of evidence which needs to be examined in the context of other evidence.' A major aim of this work was to simply find another powerful way of giving young people a voice. YPSA, unlike British Social Attitudes, will not run every year, but it took place again in 1998, run by SCPR and funded by the ESRC.

While market researchers and pollsters have been quick off the mark in understanding the importance of listening to children, academic researchers have been slower to grasp the need to work directly with young people – a caution which may have a basis in important methodological, ethical and other concerns. The issue of whether children can be reliable respondents sits alongside the question of whether they should be. Alderson's (1993, 1995) work suggests that they are able to participate in an informed way in research, and that we as adults, practitioners, researchers and policy-makers have a great deal to learn from them. We probably know rather less about what their views are on the matter of participation.

Thus, in terms of these ethical and practical issues, those of us setting up YPSA were relieved to find that this first survey (Roberts and Sachdev 1996) demonstrated that children and young people were both willing and able to respond in a thoughtful way to a relatively sophisticated attitude survey. If they are willing to give their views on subjects on which they are, in a sense, 'experts', such as family life and education, we (that is 'we' in the broadest sense, including politicians, government departments, service providers and others) should be willing to listen to what they have to say, and incorporate their views into our understandings of what it is to be a child or young person. Without asking children and young people for their views directly, it is all too easy to fall into imputing views to them, and stereotyping 'youth' on the basis of small samples or anecdotes.

Ex cathedra statements on the young are commonplace, and there have been a number of ad-hoc studies and regular reports, such as the Walls pocket money survey (Bird's Eye Walls 1995), which have given a snapshot of family life in Britain or the views of young people. Childhood and youth are not simply a preparation for adulthood and much of the strength of the data collected rest on the unique picture they help us construct of the social attitudes of young people who are so frequently judged on the basis of sketch and stereotype. Furnham and Gunter's (1989) *Anatomy of Adolescence*, based on a sample of National Association of Youth Club members interviewed during 1985 as part of International Youth Year, is a classic, and is referred to by a number of contributors to the YPSA report. We also wanted to link the survey to a campaign Barnardo's was running: Give Us a Break, which aimed to give young people from Barnardo's projects across the UK the opportunity to speak out on issues which affect them. Issues such as the rehabilitation of young offenders, the importance of promoting safe lifestyles, youth homelessness and the lack of opportunities for school leavers were highlighted at the launch of the report at Planet Hollywood. The report, and the lack of a voice for young people, was further raised in a variety of forums, including the All Party Parliamentary Group on Children. It was part of a climate of change, in which children and young people are more frequently being asked their views.

Children Without a Voice

There are some groups of children literally or metaphorically without a voice. In the case of our Young People's Social Attitudes survey for instance, since it was based on households, it systematically excluded children on the street, children in residential schools and it almost certainly under-represented those children and young people who spend an absolute minimum of time in the parental home, for whatever reason. Some school surveys exclude those children who have problems completing a questionnaire, and very profoundly disabled children are excluded as participants from almost all research. Other children and young people, such as those who are roofless, though they may be excluded from household surveys, are so frequently asked by researchers or journalists to account for themselves and give their stories that this has become a trade for the young people as well as for the professionals. This means that we may have an abundance of information from disabled children on what it means to be disabled, and from homeless young people on living on the street, but we know far less about their views on issues which affect all young people. 'Inclusion' for them, ironically enough, can mean inclusion on the basis of their participating in surveys or research entirely focused on precisely those issues which exclude them. Disabled children and young people are more than their impairment, just as homeless young people have views on issues other than homelessness. There are, however, signs of progress here too as the examples below illustrate.

On the inclusion side, Jenny Morris has completed a piece of work for the Joseph Rowntree Foundation which included disabled children, sometimes with severe communication problems, including those with no speech. Specialist interviewers were used, and lessons learned (Morris 1998a). Some of the lessons from this have been drawn into a policy think piece for Barnardo's on the rights of disabled children to the kinds of services which all children should be able to expect (Morris 1998b).

In relation to researching roofless young people on their needs, one of my own research colleagues recently persuaded a local authority who had asked us to interview young people on the streets about what would make their lives better, that given the sound work already done in this area, and the needs amply demonstrated time after time, resources would be better spent in using what we already know to provide services and resources for young people in this situation, rather than deferring action until more knowledge could be created.

There are, of course, considerable theoretical, practical and ethical problems involved in including children and young people who have systematically been excluded from the domains where they might otherwise have a voice, and we need to be clear when it is appropriate for us to ask young people to donate time – one of their few resources – to researchers, and when it is not.

Child Protection

A particular issue which needs a good deal of further thought by all of us who interact with children, as researchers practitioners or indeed as citizens is the question of child protection. In Morris's research (referred to above), the reference group of young disabled people advising the project, all of whom had had experience of residential care, said that unless the researchers guaranteed confidentiality, people would not tell them about abuse. The research interviewers, however, some of whom had experience of child protection work, felt they could not give such a guarantee, particularly if the abuse was still taking place, or the abuser was in a position to abuse other children. It was agreed that near the beginning of each interview, the researcher would say something like:

Sometimes a person might talk about a situation where they have been harmed by someone. If this happens, I may need to talk to someone else, especially if it is something awful which is still happening to you, or if the person who harmed you may still be hurting someone else. I would want to be able to agree with you what should be done, and who should be told.

The response of one young man to this was, 'Well, that's one part of my life I'm not going to be able to talk to you about then, isn't it? I'm not having you deciding who to go and talk to about me' (Morris 1998a: 55).

Conclusion

On the basis of a number of examples, this chapter has drawn attention to some of the ways in which children and young people can be, and have been, involved in the research process. Encouraging children's participation in research is in some quarters now seen as a *sine qua non* of a pro-child stance. But the reasons why a child or young person should choose to participate in research are clearer in some studies than others. While it is likely that research on children which includes children and young people will considerably strengthen some aspects of the research, we cannot take it for granted that participation in research, and the development of increasingly sophisticated research methods to facilitate children's participation is necessarily always in their interests. What serves a research agenda does not always fulfil a policy or practice agenda, or further a participant's interests. Childhood is not simply a preparation for adult life, and we cannot assume that those issues we as researchers, or practitioners, or policy-makers find gripping will hold quite the same interest for children and young people. However careful we are about informed consent, there are aspects of the adult–child relationship or practical issues concerning research in schools or youth settings which may make non-participation difficult for a child or young person. For this reason, I believe that there is an onus on us to make participation in research, at whatever level, an experience which is at best fun, and at worst, does no harm, to young people. The time that they devote to our research agendas is a gift, and one which we should be prepared to reciprocate. In considering the inclusion of children in research, we need to be thoughtful in terms of which particular research horse is appropriate for which particular policy course. There are some policy or practice related research questions for which the child's voice is entirely appropriate; others, for instance those relating to fiscal policies as they affect children, where it is likely that the child's voice would be no more than illustrative.

It is clear that listening to children, hearing children, and acting on what children say are three very different activities, although they are frequently elided as if they were not. The (re)discovery of children in the academy is akin in some respects to the rediscovery of poverty, of women, or of the working class in the 1960s and 1970s. Children have always been with us (Zelizer 1986). There have always been people who have listened, sometimes there have been people who have heard, and perhaps less often, those who have acted wisely on what children have had to say.

References

Alderson, P. (1993) *Children's Consent to Surgery*, Buckingham: Open University Press.

Alderson, P. (1995) *Listening to Children: Children, Ethics and Social Research*, Barkingside: Barnardo's.

Ash, A., Bellew, J., Davies, M., Newman, T. and Richardson, L. (1997a) *Everybody In?*, Barkingside: Barnardo's.

Ash, A., Bellew, J., Davies, M., Newman, T. and Richardson, L. (1997b) 'Everybody in? The experience of disabled students in colleges of further education', *Disability and Society*, 12(4): 605–21.

Barnardo's (1998) *Whose Daughter Next? Children Abused through Prostitution*, Barkingside: Barnardo's.

Bird's Eye Walls (1995) *Walls Monitor*, London: Bird's Eye Walls.

Brook, L. (1996) *British Social Attitudes: Young People's Social Attitudes and Northern Ireland Social Attitudes 1994 Surveys*, London: Social and Community Planning Research.

Cohen, R., Hughes, M. with Ashworth, L. and Blair, M. (1994) *School's Out: The Family Perspective on School Exclusion*, Barkingside: Barnardo's.

Downes, D. and Rock, P. (1990) Preface to J. Davis, *Youth and the Condition of Britain, Images of Adolescent Conflict*, London: Athlone.

Doyle, A. (1875) *Pauper Children (Canada)*, Return to an Order of the Honourable The House of Commons dated 8 February 1875.

Furnham, A. and Gunter, B. (1989) *Young People's Social Attitudes in Britain: The Anatomy of Adolescence*, London: Routledge.

Graham, H. (1983) 'Do her answers fit his questions?': Women and the survey method,' in E. Gamarnikow, D. Morgan, J. Purvis and D. Taylorson (eds) *The Public and the Private*, London: Heinemann.

Graham, H. (1984) 'Surveying through stories', in C. Bell and H. Roberts (eds) *Social Researching: Politics, Problems, Practice*, London: Routledge and Kegan Paul.

Grodin, M. and Glantz, L. (1994) *Children and Research Subjects: Science, Ethics and Law*, Oxford: Oxford University Press.

Hurley, N. (1998) *Straight Talk: Working with Children and Young People in Groups*, York: Joseph Rowntree Foundation.

Imrie, J. and Coombes, Y. (1995) *No Time to Waste: The Scale and Dimensions of the Problem of Children Affected by HIV/AIDs in the United Kingdom*, Barkingside: Barnardo's.

Jowell, R. (1984) 'Introducing the survey', in R. Jowell and C. Airey (eds) *British Social Attitudes: The 1984 Report*, Aldershot: Gower.

Jowell, R. and Airey, C. (1984) *British Social Attitudes: The 1984 Report*, Aldershot: Gower.

McNeish, D. (1993) *Liquid Gold: The Cost of Water in the 90s*, Barkingside: Barnardo's.

Morris, J. (1998a) *Still Missing?*, vol. 1, *The Experience of Disabled Children Living Apart from their Families*, London: Who Cares Trust.

Morris, J. (1998b) *Accessing Human Rights: Disabled Children and the Children Act*, Barkingside: Barnardo's.

Newman, T. (1996) 'Rights, rites and responsibilities: the age of transition to the adult world', in H. Roberts and D. Sachdev (eds) *Young People's Social Attitudes*, Barkingside: Barnardo's.

Oakley, A. (1981) 'Interviewing women: a contradiction in terms', in H. Roberts (ed.) *Doing Feminist Research*, London: Routledge and Kegan Paul.

Roberts, H. and Sachdev, D. (eds) (1996) *Young People's Social Attitudes*, Barkingside: Barnardo's.

Sellick, C. and Thoburn, J. (1996) *What Works in Family Placement?*, Barkingside: Barnardo's.

Selltiz, C., Jahoda, M., Deutsch, M. and Cook, S.W. (1965) *Research Methods in Social Relations*, London: Methuen.

Sjoberg, G. and Nett, R. (1968) *A Methodology for Social Research*, New York: Harper and Row.

Turner, C.F. and Martin, E. (eds) (1981) *Surveys of Subjective Phenomena: A Summary Report*, Washington, DC: National Academy Press.

Ward, L. (1997) *Seen and Heard: Involving Disabled Children and Young People in Research Projects*, York: Joseph Rowntree Foundation.

Zelizer, V.A. (1986) *Pricing the Priceless Child*, New York: Basic Books.

12 Children as Researchers

The Effects of Participation Rights on Research Methodology

Priscilla Alderson

Introduction

Increasingly, children are being involved as researchers, and this chapter considers issues raised for adults who do research with child researchers. The points will be illustrated through a review of an international literature rather than an original research report. Three main areas will be discussed: stages of the research process at which children can be involved as actors; levels of children's participation; and the use of methods which can increase children's informed involvement in research, thereby respecting their rights. The idea of seeing the researched adult as a co-researcher or co-producer of data, and equally involved in the analysis, is already widely acknowledged. This idea is usually argued for in terms of control, and of addressing power imbalances in the research relationship. It can also be justified in terms of efficiency, as opening the way to a broader range of collection methods and fuller understanding of the data. This chapter, similarly, sees children as co-producers of data during research conducted with them.

An explicit and implicit theme within this type of co-research is respect for the researched group and for their own views and abilities. Respect links closely to rights, and rights conventions offer a principled, yet flexible, means of justifying and extending respectful practices (Spencer 1998). Rights conventions which have near-universal support and quasi-legal status therefore provide formal justification for observing ethical standards in research. This growing awareness of the rights of children, and other minority groups including women, has paved the way for involving children as researchers.

Internationally, children's rights have taken on a new dimension since the late 1980s with the so-called participation rights. Traditionally, children have been excluded from what are known as the first generation or autonomy rights: freedom from interference and rights to physical and mental integrity and self-determination. Instead, children were assumed to be under their parents' protection and control. International declarations of

241

children's rights, initially concerned with war victims, stressed their needs for protection from neglect and abuse and for provision of goods and services. Until recently, research about children has reflected these priorities, mainly by measuring the effects of health or education interventions in their lives, or their needs as assessed by adults, or investigating their gradual development and socialization towards adult competence.

However, the new dimension of children's participation rights, enshrined in the UN Convention on the Rights of the Child 1989 (United Nations 1989), involves moderate versions of adult autonomy rights. They concern children taking part, in activities and decisions which affect them. Participation rights include especially three of the Convention's 54 articles. State parties should assure:[1]

the child who is capable of forming his or her own views the right to express those views freely in all matters affecting the child, the views of the child being given due weight in accordance with the age and maturity of the child (12);

the right to freedom of expression [including] freedom to seek, review and impart information and ideas of all kinds . . . through any other media of the child's choice (13);

the right of the child to rest and leisure, to engage in play and . . . cultural life and the arts (31).

The rights are qualified in important ways. Some, for example, are aspirational, not yet fully realizable, but only 'to the maximum extent of [each nation's] available resources' (4). The rights are also not absolute but conditional, affected by the 'evolving capacities of the child', the 'responsibilities, rights and duties of parents' (5) and the national law. 'The best interests of the child must be the primary consideration' (1, 21). Children's rights cannot be exercised in ways which would harm the child or other people. They must 'respect the rights and reputations of others', as well as 'national security and public order, health and morals' (13). The rights are not about selfish individualism but about solidarity, social justice and fair distribution. To claim a right is to acknowledge that everyone else has an equal claim to it. The claim affirms the worth and dignity of every person. Respect for children's rights promotes 'social progress and better standards of life in larger freedom' (preamble of the Convention).

Every government except the United States and Somalia has ratified the Convention, undertaking to publicize it 'to adults and children alike', to bring state laws and services to accord with it, and to report regularly to the UN on progress in doing so. Yet children's rights remain problematic with controversies about how participation rights can complement yet also conflict with provision and protection rights (Alderson and Goodwin 1993).

In these controversies, there are several influences which have altered the status of children in research, and as researchers, during the 1990s, for instance: the aftermath of the Gillick ruling in 1985 that children aged under 16 can give valid consent (for a review see Alderson and Montgomery 1996); new respect in the sociology of childhood for children as competent social actors, who are no longer seen as simply subsumed under adult-dominated headings like the family (Qvortrup et al. 1994; James and Prout 1997); the well-publicized eloquence of young children, for example, on television. Importantly, for this chapter, there is also research by children themselves, which has been largely sponsored by non-governmental organizations (NGOs) in accordance with the UN Convention, and which will be considered in the rest of this chapter.

Issues Which Children's Rights Raise for Adult Researchers

Children's participation involves a changing emphasis in research methods and topics. Recognizing children as subjects rather than objects of research entails accepting that children can speak 'in their own right' and report valid views and experiences. Such 'speaking' may involve sign language when children cannot hear or talk, and other expressive body language and sounds, such as those made by children with autism and severe learning difficulties (Alderson and Goodey 1998). To involve all children more directly in research can therefore rescue them from silence and exclusion, and from being represented, by default, as passive objects, while respect for their informed and voluntary consent helps to protect them from covert, invasive, exploitative or abusive research.

This latter point is important, for one major obstacle in conducting research with children concerns infantilizing them, perceiving and treating them as immature and, in so doing, producing evidence to reinforce notions of their incompetence. This can include 'talking down' to children by using over-simple words and concepts, restricting them into making only superficial responses, and involving only inexperienced children and not those with intense relevant experience who could give much more informed responses. For example, children's views about illness and medical treatments are frequently collected from average samples of mainly healthy children (Wilkinson 1988). They appear to be relatively ignorant, despite information they may have gained from television and other sources. Children who have chronic illness, on the other hand, will have far greater knowledge about the nature and purpose of medical treatments; 2 year olds with cancer can talk with great understanding that challenges beliefs about their inability to understand (Kendrick 1986).

Alternatively, researchers' over-complicated or poorly explained terms, topics and methods can also misleadingly make children (and some adults) appear to be ignorant or incapable. Children may help adult researchers to set more appropriate levels of talk (Solberg 1997; see also O'Kane, Chapter 7). During research about children's consent to surgery, I asked a 10-year-old girl, 'So you are having your legs made longer?' and she replied, 'I suffer from achondroplasia and I am having my femurs lengthened,' politely showing me her sophisticated level of talk and insight (Alderson 1993).

Another obstacle for children is the common assumption by adults that the consent of parents or teachers will suffice, and that children need not or cannot express their own consent or refusal to take part in research. The British Education Research Association (BERA 1992) does not even mention children's consent in its ethical guidelines. Social research can therefore contribute to the extensive debate about children's consent (for a review see Alderson 1995), by providing evidence of children's competence in their daily life and in research (for example, in Hutchby and Moran-Ellis 1998). In the sociology of childhood, it is now commonplace to assert that children are and must be seen as actors in the social construction and determination of their own lives, the lives of those around them and of their society. Two related questions therefore arise. First, if children's social relations and culture are worthy of study in their own right, then who is better qualified to research some aspects of their lives than children themselves (James and Prout 1997)? Second, if children can be active participants, as this chapter considers, can they also be active researchers?

Children as Researchers

One way in which children are researchers is in the everyday projects that children do at school. In schools I have visited, for example, Adam (aged 5) made a graph about pets owned by children in his class, and Helen (aged 16) tape-recorded interviews with her friends about their parents' divorce for her A level psychology project. Tariq's geography GCSE project was about the local allotments threatened with closure and involved him in checking local authority records and observing a council meeting. Classes of 9 to 11 year olds watched a video about ponds, then had a brain-storming circle time and small group discussions to plan and draw a pond for their school playground. They worked to a budget and with adults' help created and stocked the pond.

In these examples, learning, the main occupation for everyone at school, overlaps with research, but this wealth of research in British schools is almost entirely unpublished, and tends to be seen as 'practising' rather than as worthwhile in its own right. In contrast, comparable activities may be highly valued in other societies, as shown in the next example.

Many Ugandan children are the first generation to attend school and they become research and health educators for the community. Through the Child-to-Child Trust which promotes peer education, the 600 children at a village primary school became concerned that animals used the main well-pond. The children spoke with the village leader, who called a meeting at which the children presented poems and dramas about the value of clean water. As a result, children and adults worked together on cleaning the well-pond and building a fence to keep out the animals (International Save the Children Alliance (ISCA) 1995: 236).

The second most usual way in which children are involved in research is in projects designed and conducted by adults (see O'Kane, Chapter 7; Christensen and James, Chapter 8; Davis et al., Chapter 10; Roberts, Chapter 11). However, besides providing data in their traditional role as research subjects, increasingly, children help to plan questions, and collect, analyse or report evidence, or publicize the findings. For example, on an accident-prone estate,

> teenagers had little to say about the kinds of events we [the researchers] had thought of as accidents. Nor did they respond well to the notion of safety or safe-keeping. In the end we asked them what our opening question should be. 'Ask us about our scars', they replied. So we did, and it resulted in animated and detailed information about a number of accident events.
>
> (Roberts et al. 1995: 34)

The teenagers' initial responses could easily have been used to confirm assumptions about their ignorance and incompetence. In contrast, the part-nership approach helped to develop new theories and methods for research about accidents and their prevention, and produced conclusions, and further projects with younger children.

Indeed, children are possibly more likely than adults to be interested in every stage of research. Many of them are used to enquiring, scrutinizing, accepting unexpected results, revising their ideas, and assuming that their knowledge is incomplete and provisional. Preschool children frequently ask basic questions about philosophy and method and by 5 years have worked out understandings which last a lifetime (Lipman 1993; Tizard and Hughes 1984; Gardner 1993). Very young children can also share in making group decisions and agreeing on priorities (Miller 1997). Children may have less to lose, and more to gain, by asking radical questions, such as 'Why do we have school assembly?' Adults, by contrast, can feel threatened by research which might critically question their own expertise, authority or convenience.

The third and less common but expanding area is research which is mainly initiated and directed by children and teenagers (West 1997; PEG 1998a,

1998b). Methods of involving unschooled adults as researchers, such as through participatory rural appraisal (Pratt and Loizos 1992), are also used effectively with and by children (Johnson and Ivan-Smith 1996; see also O'Kane, Chapter 7, and Christensen and James, Chapter 8).The following sections review the stages, levels and methods through which children are involved as researchers.

Stages of Research When Children are Involved

Research in schools and universities, when the main object is to add to knowledge, tends to concentrate on the middle stages: collecting and analysing data and writing reports. In contrast, research by young people themselves, which is concerned with achieving changes in, for example, access, opportunities or the way services are provided, often also emphasizes the early and follow-up stages of the research process. The early stages include selecting and setting up the research team and sample groups, avoiding tokenism, working out team and power relationships and ways of resolving problems as they arise, jointly deciding the agenda, aims, methods and payments in cash or in kind (for example, Cockburn et al. 1997). These important initial decisions are often taken for granted in hierarchical professional research teams.

Children and teenagers also tend to be deeply concerned from the start with the follow up stages of publicity and using research findings to change the world. 'We want to show this to the social workers/planning officers/Department for Education' may be explicit initial aims (PEG, and Allan Siddall, personal communication). The national movement of street children in Brazil, for example, during the late 1980s, influenced the drafting of legal codes ranging from the new federal constitution to municipal laws which enshrine children's rights based on research they had conducted (Save the Children Fund (SCF) 1995). The following examples illustrate ways in which young people work at various stages of research.

The Participation and Education Group (PEG 1998a) researched how unhealthy schools can be. The replies to the 14 questions, from 187 young people aged from 5 to 25, vividly combine physical with mental health: 'If you can't do the work you get picked on and called thick. You feel sick and bad.' The lively research report includes graphs and pie charts, poems, quotations and makes strong recommendations. PEG also made dramatic presentations about its research to health professionals, and at the Department for Education and Employment. PEG uses equal opportunity methods promoted in assertion training and by rights workers (Treseder 1997). PEG members' assertiveness, after only brief training, challenges assumptions that children and young people are inevitably vulnerable. For example, some of the youngest members drew up the agenda and chaired a meeting of young people aged from 8 years and adults, to plan a conference. They stated the rules of listening with respect, and the adults were politely reminded not to interrupt or talk down to children, and everyone had a turn to speak to questions such as: Why are we having this meeting? What did you get out of the meeting? (PEG 1998b).

In Camden, London, Bangladeshi teenagers researched the play and leisure needs of Bangladeshi children, and young children shared in designing and developing the project to ensure that it took accurate account of their perspectives which are literally a low-down child's eye view (Howarth 1997). The young researchers used qualitative and quantitative methods, with focus groups, an audit of play provision, interviews with 83 8–12 year olds, and with parents, head teachers and community workers. They discovered why so few children used public play facilities and recommended how to make them more safe and attractive.

In another community project, children aged 3 to 8 years used cameras and conducted surveys and interviews about children's views on improving their housing estate. They published an illustrated report, which six of them presented and discussed with local authority officers at a 'proper' meeting round a table. Some of their recommendations were used, such as having the playground in the centre of the estate, not on the edge, and beyond busy peripheral roads as the adults had planned (Miller 1997).

Young people also help to disseminate research memorably. At a conference of over two hundred health professionals which I attended in 1994, seven teenagers presented accounts and poems. First, they asked the attenders to put their hands over their ears. This lasted for over a minute and felt much longer. Smiles among the audience began to change into bewilderment. At last the teenagers said, 'Now you can take your hands away. You ask us what it is like for us when we talk to health workers. That is usually what it is like.' Another instance of the drama and immediacy which young people's presentations can have occurred at a Barnardo's conference to launch the research report on *Listening to Children* (Alderson 1995). Five teenagers, dressed all in black, presented a short play in which they wove the Hansel and Gretel story and French mime techniques into a sombre, poignant depiction of children's despair at not being heard. Although I had written the report, and spoke at the conference, all my nervousness was concentrated on the actors. Would they actually turn up? What were they going to do? Would it be an appalling flop? Would we hurt the young people, and the whole message of the day, by entrusting so much responsibility to them? It is risky to ask inexperienced and traditionally unheard young people to appear at daunting public meetings, and to give much more than a typical speech, and it is hard to overcome adult anxieties about this. In the event, the play succeeded in influencing the hearts and minds of policy-makers. After prolonged applause, the director of Barnardo's thanked them and then invited questions about earlier sessions. After a long silence, a senior Department of Health official said that he thought everyone was too deeply impressed by the play to talk about other topics.

Levels of Children's Involvement

The term 'child-centred research' loosely covers methods, stages or levels of children's involvement (Connolly and Ennew 1996). Although methods involving games may appear child-friendly, a crucial aspect is the level at which adults share or hold back knowledge and control from children. The different levels of control-sharing and of children's participation have been compared, for example, with rungs on a ladder (Arnstein 1979; Hart 1992). At the lowest levels is the pretence of shared work: manipulation, decoration and tokenism. The next levels involve actual participation: children being assigned to tasks although being informed and consulted; and adults initiating but also sharing decisions with children. The top two levels concern projects more fully initiated and directed by children.

The ladder image can be a useful guide towards assessing how far children are or could be participating with the interpersonal and structural barriers to be overcome. One main barrier is the way that funders seldom fund the important initial and follow up stages of research described earlier as so important to young people. Ways of involving children more fully in making policy decisions have been extensively reported (Lorenzo 1992; Miller 1997; Wellard et al. 1997). However, levels of children's participation are also affected by children's capacity to understand the relevant issues. Can young children, for example, understand critical analysis, or the politics of racism? A report by a teacher suggests that the 7 year olds she taught could do so (Butler 1998). She describes how black children in downtown Chicago became conscious of racial, economic and political oppressions, as they discussed their own experiences intensely in class. If someone wanted to talk about rocks or ants or something not obviously related to justice, they would say, 'That's nice, but what does that have to do with peace and power?' 'How you gonna help your Brothers and Sisters by talking about that?' They analysed contradictions between the rhetoric and reality in their lives, the social pressures that restrict individual agency, and how they can work for social justice, power, unity and community change.

Methods Used by Young Researchers

Children working as researchers use many methods, singly or in groups, with or without adults. They select research topics, general questions and methods, decide specific survey questions or interview topics, and select respondents and observation sites. Some conduct pilots and revise their plans, and plan the data collection, collation and analysis. After the analysis by hand or computer, they write reports and disseminate the findings, and discuss them with policy-makers (for example, SCF 1997; SCF and Kirklees Metropolitan Council 1996; Ash et al. 1997; Beresford 1997; Wellard et al. 1997; PEG 1998a, 1998b). Research reports by young groups range from long typed reports (West 1997) to a simple poster or wall newspaper, a video or photographic exhibition, with reports and drawings by the whole team or from smaller groups (Howarth 1997; Johnson et al. 1996). School projects have included producing a video and exhibition on a town's facilities for disabled people; and surveying and proposing new road safety measures which were built. Children have also been involved in projects ranging from improving architectural designs for a new children's hospital in Derby, to working on anti-poverty measures in Greenwich (all in Willow 1997). One group reviewed multicultural policies in their school, designed and presented a policy to the student council, and planned in-service training sessions for school governors and staff with a local race relations group (Centre for Citizenship Studies in Education (CCSE) no date).

Some young children seem to be able to understand complex methods. For example, Emily Rosa (aged 9) designed an elegant randomized trial of 21 therapeutic touch healers who took part in 280 tests. They put their hands through holes in a screen 30 cm apart, and Emily spun a coin to determine whether she would hold her hands just above their left or right hand. The aim was to show whether the healers were aware of the kinds of human energy fields through which they claim to heal. Accuracy would have to be well above 50 per cent to demonstrate sensitivity, but was only 47 per cent in the first trial and 41 per cent in the second. Emily's mother believed that the healers took part because they did not feel threatened by a child, and experts praised this simple and novel way of gaining evidence that casts strong doubt on the healers' claims. Previously, complicated, lengthy and expensive trials had compared patients' healing rates after therapeutic touch and more orthodox treatments (Rosa 1988).

Young researchers around England have used Open College training materials to conduct ambitious projects. School girls investigating children's participation rights decided to interview the directors of education, social and leisure services, the chief executives and council leaders and some assistant chief constables in six north-east local authorities. They practised tape-recording and taking notes during interviews with their teachers and a research officer who later debriefed them. In pairs, they piloted interviews with a senior researcher who thought they were 'brilliant' and that he would not have been able to arrange the access which they achieved – they had only one refusal (Allan Siddall, personal communication). The girls discussed the merits of qualitative and quantitative methods when analysing their interviews, and considered how their evidence clearly showed that the officers' rhetoric did not fit the reality. They presented their work

(Nevison 1997), which now influences local policies, at a launch and at national conferences.

In another project, care leavers aged 16 years and older investigated experiences of young people leaving care in five British cities. This group is highly over-represented among the homeless and prison population. The young researchers chose the research topics and questions during five residential meetings, and interviewed eighty young care leavers and twenty-two social work staff. They undertook full qualitative analysis of the results and made recommendations based on these. They worked on writing and launching the report and talked to the media. Later they talked to local authorities about the work, and made a video (West 1997). Another project combined different teams with a central research group, and flexible use of core questions on twelve research sites. A key coordinating worker liaised with one practitioner and two young people on each site, and all of them made up the research group which took overall control over methods and editing of reports. They identified the main themes and twenty questions per theme. They worked mainly in schools, but also with groups of refugees and homeless young people (Kenny and Cockburn 1997).

Another example of methods used by children is textual analysis. On the *Children's Express*, the reporters (aged 8–13) conduct penetrating interviews, and the editors are aged 14–18. Most of them come from backgrounds which offer them few opportunities, and they publish reports in many newspapers and magazines. Recently, twenty-seven of them monitored four hundred stories in the national press to find that every article stereotyped children – as victims, cute, evil, exceptionally excelling, corrupted, as accessories to adults or as 'brave little angels'. They held a conference in 1998, Kids These Days, to publicize their research (Neustatter 1998).

Research and Play

A striking aspect of children's research is the combining of work and play. Young researchers use ice-breaking sessions to help one another to feel confident and relaxed, more willing to listen to one another and to risk sharing ideas with less fear of being dismissed (Johnson et al. 1996; Treseder 1997). The UN Convention links rights to engage in cultural life with the right to play (Article 31) resonating with the way play methods can enhance children's research imagination. For example, talking about 'let's pretend' can involve young children in planning improvements in playgrounds and nurseries (Miller 1997). Similarly, one lively, well-illustrated pack produced with children shows how to promote genuine participation, negotiation and power sharing through games, with details on promoting equal opportunities and chat space methods (SCF and Kirklees 1996). The play approaches help research teams to enjoy being together as well as working together, and help to sustain the enthusiasm of children who are usually volunteers. Young children can be good at listening, questioning, challenging, keeping to the point, and helping each other to learn and develop ideas (McNamara and Moreton 1997; see also O'Kane, Chapter 7). For example, adults with young children select topics and ideas and note them in words or pictures on large sheets and everyone has coloured sticky dots to put beside the most liked items. This provides an instant relatively anonymous evaluation for everyone to see at a glance. It is one of several democratic, quick and fun ways to assess opinions. Very young or illiterate children can contribute detailed data through their songs and dreams, by models, drawings or maps about their daily mobility and routines (Johnson et al. 1996; Boyden and Ennew 1997) or about their local wild life (Hart 1992).

Research and Work

It has been argued that children's work mirrors adults' work, in being mainly either physical or mental labour (Qvortrup 1998). European and north American societies tend to identify work, and therefore research, with mental effort. In cultures where the emphasis is more on physical work, the next examples could be seen as action research, because knowledge is gained through learning from difficulties, planning projects, collecting and applying new knowledge, publicizing the research products (food and news) and testing public responses. In one example, during their monthly meetings, street boys in New Delhi realized that they spent 75 per cent of their money on food and they planned their project. Twelve boys, aged 7 to 17, took an intensive ten day course on cooking, nutrition, cleanliness, looking after customers and book-keeping, and they had help with renting a space for a restaurant. They took half pay at first, saying 'You can't expect to be an over-night success in this business, one has to bear losses for a while . . . and try very hard'. They gave free food to some street children, learned Chinese cooking to expand the menu, and planned to raise money to buy a van to take food to an area where there are many street children, financed by selling snacks in public places (ISCA 1995: 239).

In a comparable example, in Sarajevo in 1993, eighteen editors aged 10–13 years ran a radio programme, *Colourful Wall*, with an estimated audience of 80 per cent of all the local citizens. They conducted polls of children's views and based their programme planning on the results. They had fifteen press centres through the city to which children brought news items, and when the phones were working these were phoned through to the radio station. Many schools were closed at the time, and many children were injured and bereaved. The programme carried education, entertainment and psychological support for them, with counsellors, a personal column section and a daily slot on children's rights. The young disc jockeys were especially popular and, like the New Delhi boys, were keen to evaluate and expand their work.

Practical Problems for Child Researchers

However, problems and questions arise for child researchers, as they do for adult 'lay' researchers (Pratt and Loizos 1992) and for children who are the subjects of research (Alderson 1995). How can young researchers work with adults on reasonably equal, informed and unpressured terms? How much responsibility is it fair to expect children to carry and how much should adults intervene to support them or to control the research? How can adults avoid exploiting or manipulating children, as in the participation ladders mentioned earlier? How much time can children be expected to give to research beyond the work they may already do at school, at home or outside the home, or begging? Should they be paid and, if so, how much, and in cash or in kind? There can be further problems with research expenses, and access to research meetings for children who have to have an adult escort. When research is conducted through schools, teachers may need to be, or insist on being, involved and this can set up new adult–child power imbalances to attend to. When child researchers seem to be over-impressed with, for example, the views of officials which they have collected, should adults encourage them to be more critical? And who should have final control over the data and any reports, the children or adult or both jointly?

Journalists, for example, may be more willing to publicize research by children, but may also misreport them, as they misreport some adults' research. A junior school was praised in the *Guardian* for its hard-won innovations (Highfield School 1997), but these were disparaged in the local newspaper. When the children complained to the editor he refused to respond, so every child in the school wrote a letter to fax to him. After his fax had been jammed for some hours, the editor agreed to accept their public right of reply. The head teacher believed that they were exercising their democratic rights as citizens.

I have mentioned just a few from many potential complications to show that working with child researchers does not simply resolve problems of power, exploitation or coercion. Indeed it may amplify them and so working methods need to be planned, tested, evaluated and developed with the young researchers. One advantage of working in a research team with them is that there is more time to talk, than there can be with child research subjects, and to turn problems into opportunities for children and adults to increase their skill and knowledge.

Conclusion: Working with Child Researchers

The growing literature on children as researchers suggests that children are an underestimated, underused resource. Just as research about women has become far more insightful because women are involved as researchers, the scope of research about children could be expanded by involving children as researchers in many methods, levels and stages of the process. Children are the primary source of knowledge about their own views and experiences. They can be a means of access to other children, including those who may be protected from strange adults. The novelty and immediacy of children's research reports can attract greater publicity and interest in using the findings than much adult research does. Doing research helps children (perhaps disadvantaged ones especially) to gain more skills, confidence and perhaps determination to overcome their disadvantages than adult researchers working on their behalf could give them. Adult researchers have noted their surprise at child researchers' competence, and mentioned their plans to do more complicated work and work with younger children in future. Adult researchers frequently emphasize the value of listening to children, and this point is made more effectively when children can express themselves through doing and publicly reporting their own research.

Today, new political and funding pressures promote research by children. NGOs follow international guidance that their own research and services should be child-focused, strongly and directly influenced by children, in accordance with the 1989 UN Convention. Governments, having ratified the Convention, should also be doing so through all their agencies. As more children's research is published, the dangers of ignoring their views (Cooter 1992), and the benefits of working with them become more obvious. Funding bodies like the ESRC and the Joseph Rowntree Foundation expect researchers to work closely with user groups, from inception to the implementation stages of research. Although this has potential disadvantages when powerful commercial or professional bodies prevent researchers from being adventurous, independent and critical, consulting children as the largest user group of research affecting them can redress inter-generation imbalances of power. As the examples have shown, work by young researchers can open up new directions for research, and respect children's rights.

A booklet for young people 'whose sense of adventure and idealism is the only hope for more voluntary action in future against unsavoury acts towards humans and Nature' quotes Gandhi: 'My humble occupation has been to show people how they can solve their own difficulties' (Oza 1991). NGOs work with child researchers to improve understanding of children's lives, their interests, concerns, capacities and needs; to see them in the context of their family, community and society; to demonstrate children's ability to take part in research, their competencies, ingenuity and originality.

They show how children can have unique and valid perspectives to inform social policy (SCF 1997: 2–5) and to help towards solving their own difficulties.

Finally, the vogue for excluding as researchers people who are personally affected by the research topic for fear of bias has largely been superseded by respect for researchers with inside knowledge. All the arguments proposed by feminist and black researchers supporting their research about their own group also apply to children. Postmodern deconstruction of subjectivity sees it

> as a product of power rather than its author; and [sees] agency as power's way of acting through the individual. [Power] is not unitary and zero-sum, but diffuse, constantly changing and plural . . . The selves we think are fixed and unitary are actually unstable, fragmented and contradictory. [Postmodernism] can thus potentially help us to look at changes and tensions (such as that of oppressor/oppressed) in who we understand ourselves as being . . . The act of deconstruction is political, as it exposes the intricate operations of power that constitute subjectivity.
>
> (Aziz 1997: 76)

In research about children, a key question is: how can adults get beyond the power constraints and expose the intricacies of power in relations between adults and children? Research by children with its emphasis on addressing power before during and after the formal research stages, with its use of potentially partly subversive games, and its expansion beyond thinking into shared doing, can offer useful approaches. When I interview disabled or black people, I find that although we discuss difficulties that arise from discrimination, we are also partly papering over the cracks of these very differences in order to try to hold equal respectful relationships. In contrast, when black researchers talk with black interviewees, their common experiences of these differences enable them to explore them much more deeply (Scott 1998) and this shared exploration can apply to children's research about children.

Notions of childhood vary, and we cannot easily transfer experiences, structures and attitudes across cultures. Child researchers tend to be more adventurously involved in poor and war-torn countries, in adult work as well as research; they cannot simply set up restaurants in the UK as they can in New Delhi. The limitations in Europe and North America for research by children seem to lie less therefore in children's (in)competencies, than in adults' limiting attitudes, in constraints, and concern for protection over participation rights. However, the evidence of child researchers' activities and achievements, as well as their research findings, are likely to promote more respectful and realistic appreciation of their abilities as social actors.

Acknowledgements

I am grateful to all the young people who have helped me to do research, to the ESRC research programme, Children 5–16: Growing into the 21st Century, for funding our research on civil rights in schools which has indirectly contributed to this chapter, and to everyone who contributed many more examples of research by children than I could include here.

Note

1 Figures in parentheses refer to the relevant Article of the Convention.

References

Alderson, P. (1993) *Children's Consent to Surgery*, Buckingham: Open University Press.

Alderson, P. (1995) *Listening to Children: Children, Ethics and Social Research*, Barkingside: Barnardo's.

Alderson, P. (1999) *Young Children's Rights*, London: Save the Children Fund, Jessica Kingsley.

Alderson, P. and Goodey, C. (1998) *Enabling Education: Experiences in Special and Ordinary Schools*, London: Tufnell Press.

Alderson, P. and Goodwin, M. (1993) 'Contradictions within concepts of children's competence', *International Journal of Children's Rights* 1(3/4): 303–12.

Alderson, P. and Montgomery, J. (1996) *Health Care Choices: Making Decisions with Children*, London: Institute for Public Policy Research.

Arnstein, S. (1979) 'Eight rungs on the ladder of citizen participation', *Journal of the American Institute of Planners*, adapted by R. Hart (1992) *Children's Participation: From Tokenism to Citizenship*, Florence: Unicef.

Ash, A., Bellew, J., Davies, M., Newman, T. and Richardson, L. (1997) 'Everybody in? The experience of disabled students in further education', *Disability and Society* 12(4): 605–21.

Aziz, R. (1997) 'Feminism and the challenge of racism', in H. Mirza (ed.) *Black British Feminism*, London: Routledge.

Beresford. B. (1997) *Personal Accounts: Involving Disabled Children in Research*, York: SPRU (Social Policy Research Unit).

Boyden, J. and Ennew, J. (1997) *Children in Focus: A Manual for Participatory Research with Children*, Stockholm: Radda Barnen.

British Education Research Association (BERA) (1992) *Ethical Guidelines for Educational Research*, Slough: BERA.

Butler, M. (1998) 'Negotiating place', in S. Steinberg and J. Kincheloe (eds) *Students as Researchers*, London: Falmer Press.

Centre for Citizenship Studies in Education (CCSE) (no date) *Citizenship Education no. 31*, Leicester: Centre for Citizenship Studies in Education.

Cockburn, T., Kenny, S. and Webb, M. (1997) *Moss Side Youth Audit: Phase 2, Indicative Findings in Employment and Training*, Manchester: Manchester City Council and Manchester Metropolitan University.

Connolly, M. and Ennew, J. (eds) (1996) 'Children out of place: special issue on Working and Street Children', *Childhood* 3(2): 141–46.

Cooter, R. (1992) *In the Name of the Child*, London: Routledge.

Gardner, H. (1993) *The Unschooled Mind*, New York: Fontana.

Hart, R. (1992) *Children's Participation: From Tokenism to Citizenship*, London: Earthscan/Unicef.

Highfield School (1997) *Changing our School*, ed. P. Alderson, Plymouth and London: Highfield School and Institute of Education, University of London.

Howarth, R. (1997) *If We Don't Play Now, When Can We?*, London: Hopscotch Asian Women's Centre.

Hutchby, I. and Moran-Ellis, J. (eds) (1998) *Children and Social Competence: Arenas of Action*, London: Falmer Press.

International Save the Children Alliance (ISCA) (1995) *UN Convention on the Rights of the Child Training Kit*, London: Save the Children Fund.

James, A. and Prout, A. (eds) (1997) *Constructing and Reconstructing Childhood*, London: Falmer Press.

Johnson, V., Hill, J. and Ivan-Smith, E. (1996) *Listening to Smaller Voices: Children in an Environment of Change*, Chard: ActionAid.

Kendrick, C. (1986) 'Children's understanding of their illness and treatment within a paediatric oncology unit', *ACPP Newsletter* 8(2): 16–20.

Kenny, S. and Cockburn, T. (1997) *The Moss Side Youth Audit: Final Report*, Manchester: Manchester City Council and Manchester Metropolitan University.

Lipman, M. (ed.) (1993) *Thinking Children and Education*, Dubuque, Iowa: Kendall/ Hunt.

Lorenzo, R. (1992) *Italy: Too Little Time and Space for Childhood*, Florence: Unicef.

McNamara, S. and Moreton, G. (1997) *Understanding Differentiation: A Teacher's Guide*, London: David Fulton.

Miller, J. (1997) *Never Too Young*, London: National Early Years Network and Save the Children Fund.

Neustatter, A. (1998) 'Kids – what the papers say', *Guardian* 8 April.

Nevison, C. (1997) *A Matter of Opinion*, London: Save the Children Fund.

Oza, D. (1991) *Voluntary Action and Gandhian Approach*, New Delhi: National Book Trust India.

PEG (1998a) *Schools Can Seriously Damage your Health: How Children Think School Affects and Deals with their Health*, Gateshead: PEG.

PEG (1998b) *PEG Newsletter*, celebration issue, Gateshead: PEG.

Pratt, B and Loizos, P. (1992) *Choosing Research Methods: Data Collection for Development Workers*, Oxford: Oxfam.

Qvortrup, J. (1998) Plenary lecture to Conference on Childhood and Social Exclusion, Centre for the Social Study of Childhood, Hull, March.

Qvortrup, J., Bardy, M., Sgritta, S. and Wintersberger, H. (eds) (1994) *Childhood Matters: Social Theory, Practice and Politics*, Aldershot: Avebury.

Roberts, H., Smith, S. and Bryce, C. (1995) *Children at Risk? Safety as a Social Value*, Buckingham: Open University Press.

Rosa, E. (1988) Article in *Journal of the American Medical Association* 279: 1005–10.

Save the Children Fund (SCF) (1995) *Towards a Children's Agenda*, London. Save the Children Fund.

Save the Children Fund (1997) *Learning from Experience: Participatory Approaches in Save the Children*, London: Save the Children Fund.

Save the Children and Kirklees Metropolitan Council (1996) *The Children's Participation Pack: A Practical Guide for Play Workers*, London: Save the Children Fund.

Scott, P. (1998) 'Caribbean people's experience of diabetes', in S. Hood, B. Mayall and S. Oliver (eds) *Critical Issues in Social Research: Power and Prejudice*, Buckingham: Open University Press.

Solberg, A. (1997) 'Negotiating childhood', in A. James and A. Prout (eds) *Constructing and Reconstructing Childhood*, London, Falmer Press.

Spencer, S. (1998) 'The implications of the Human Rights Act for education', Keynote address to the fifth international summer school of the Education in Human Rights Network, Birmingham, May.

Tizard, B. and Hughes, M. (1984) *Young Children Learning*, Glasgow: Fontana.

Treseder, P. (1997) *Empowering Children and Young People: A Training Manual for Promoting Involvement in Decision-Making*, London: Save the Children Fund and Children's Rights Office.

United Nations (1989) *Convention on the Rights of the Child*, Geneva: UN.

Wellard, S., Tearse, M. and West, A. (1997) *All Together Now: Community Participation for Children and Young People*, London: Save the Children Fund.

West, A. (1997) *Learning about Leaving Care through Research by Young Care Leavers. Learning from Experience: Participatory Approaches in SCF*, London: Save the Children Fund.

Wilkinson, S. (1988) *The Child's World of Illness: The Development of Health and Illness Behaviour*, Cambridge: Cambridge University Press.

Willow, C. (1997) *Hear! Hear! Promoting Children's and Young People's Democratic Participation in Local Government*, London: Local Government Information Unit.

Notes on Contributors

Priscilla Alderson is Reader in Childhood Studies at the Institute of Education, University of London and is interested in children's competence and wisdom. Recent work includes a survey of school students' views about the UN Convention on the Rights of the Child 1989, and its effects on their lives, a comparative education study reported in *Enabling Education: Experience in Special and Mainstream Schools* (with Chris Goodey, Tufnell Press 1988) and a report for the Save the Children Fund on consulting children from birth to 8 years.

Pia Christensen is a Research Fellow and Associate Director of the Centre for the Social Study of Childhood, University of Hull. Her main interests and publications are in the anthropological study of children's everyday lives and of children's health, with a particular focus on the individual and collective actions of children. Her current research (with A. James and C. Jenks) is a study of the perception, understanding and social organization of children's time, a project funded by the ESRC Children 5–16 research programme.

William A. Corsaro is Robert H. Shaffer Class of 1967 Endowed Professor of Sociology at Indiana University, Bloomington, USA. His main interests relate to the sociology of childhood, children's peer cultures, and ethnographic research methods. He is the author of *Friendship and Peer Culture in the Early Years* (Ablex 1985) and *The Sociology of Childhood* (Pine Forge Press 1997).

Sarah Cunningham-Burley is Senior Lecturer in Medical Sociology, Department of Public Health Sciences, University of Edinburgh. Her research interests span family and medical sociology, particularly in relation to lay knowledge and experience. Her most recent work, as part of the ESRC Risk and Human Behaviour programme, examines the social and cultural impact of the new genetics with colleagues Anne Kerr and Amanda Amos.

John Davis is a Research Fellow, Department of Public Health Sciences and the Research Unit in Health and Behavioural Change, University of Edinburgh. He also works with Sarah Cunningham-Burley and Kathryn Backet-Milburn on the ESRC Health Variations project, The Socio-Economic and Cultural Context of Children's Lifestyles and the Production of Health Variations. He has a range of experience in researching sport, education and social policy and a specific interest in the use of ethnography in childhood research.

Dorothy Faulkner is a member of the Centre for Human Development and Learning at the Open University and is currently Sub-Dean Research in the School of Education at the Open University and a member of the Social Dynamics in Development and Learning research group. Her current research interests include the relationship between children's friendships and the development of social understanding and the influence of peer relationships on children's academic performance.

Harry Hendrick is a part-time lecturer in the history of childhood and youth at Oxford Brookes University. His principal publications are *Images of Youth: Age, Class and the Male Youth Problem, 1880–1920* (Clarendon 1990), *Child Welfare: England, 1872–1989* (Routledge 1994) and *Children, Childhood and English Society, 1880–1990* (Cambridge University Press 1997). He is currently working on two child health projects: children's emotional well-being in the twentieth century and child health and the development of paediatrics, 1928–75. He is writing a general history of children since the eighteenth century.

Allison James is Reader in Applied Anthropology at the University of Hull and Director of the Centre for the Social Study of Childhood. Her main research interests are in childhood, ageing and the life course. Her most recent publications are *Childhood Identities* (Edinburgh University Press 1993); *Growing Up and Growing Old* (with J. Hockey, Sage 1993) and *Theorising Childhood* (with C. Jenks and A. Prout, Polity 1998). She is currently researching children's perception and understandings of time (with P. Christensen and C. Jenks) on a project funded by the ESRC Children 5–16 research programme.

Chris Jenks is Professor of Sociology and Pro-Warden (Research) at Goldsmiths College, University of London. His most recent major publications are *Childhood* (Routledge 1996), *Theorising Childhood* (with A. James and A. Prout, Polity 1998) and *Core Sociological Dichotomies* (Sage 1998). He is currently researching children's perception and understandings of time (with P. Christensen and A. James) on a project funded by the ESRC Children 5–16 research programme.

Berry Mayall is Reader in Childhood Studies at the Institute of Education, University of London. She has carried out many studies with parents and children, with a focus on their use of services. In recent years she has worked within the new social studies of childhood. Her current study is Negotiating Childhoods, part of the ESRC Children 5–16 research programme. Her most recent books are an edited collection, *Children's Childhoods* (Falmer Press 1994) and *Children, Health and the Social Order* (Open University Press 1996).

Luisa Molinari is Researcher of Developmental Social Psychology at the Dipartimento di Scienze dell'Educazione of the University of Bologna. Her main interests concern children's relations with peers, children's rights and parental representations of children's development. She is co-author (with Francesca Emiliani) of a book on the psychological quality of life of Italian children (*Il Bambino nella Mente e nelle Parole delle Madri,* 1989) and of a book on mothers' social representations of children's development (*Rappresentazioni e Affetti,* 1995).

Claire O'Kane is a qualified social worker with experience of participatory work with children and young people, and creative training in UK and India. In the UK she worked as the researcher on the Children and Decision-Making study (University of Wales, Swansea). She is currently working as the Children's Participation Programme Officer with Butterflies Programme of Street and Working Children in Delhi, India.

Jens Qvortrup is Research Director, University of Southern Denmark Esbjerg. He has published widely on the development of a sociology of childhood and was director of the sixteen-country study, Childhood as a Social Phenomenon (1987–1993). He is past-president and founder of the Sociology of Childhood section under the ISA and is also a member of the ESRC programme board for the Children 5–16 research programme.

Helen Roberts is Coordinator of R&D with Barnardo's and honorary Senior Fellow at the Institute of Child Health and the School of Public Policy, University College London. Her main areas of interest are the evidence basis for services to children, and the ways in which we can tap into the reservoirs of expertise of children and those who care for them in developing child welfare services.

Jacqueline Scott is a member of the Faculty of Social and Political Sciences at the University of Cambridge and a fellow of Queens' College. She was formerly research director of the British Household Panel Study at Essex. Her research interests are concerned with family and household change, youth at risk, and generations and the life course. She is the principal investigator on projects funded under the ESRC programmes on Population and Household Change and Youth and Social Change.

Nick Watson is a Lecturer in Medical Sociology, Department of Nursing, University of Edinburgh. Nick has a wide range of experience in researching disability and health promotion and of working with children both as an academic and a professional in the field.

Martin Woodhead is a member of the Centre for Human Development and Learning at the Open University. He has been a Fulbright Scholar in the USA, as well as a consultant to international organizations about child development issues (e.g. Council of Europe, OECD, van Leer Foundation and Swedish Save the Children). He was series adviser to the BBC worldwide documentary television series *All Our Children*. Recent research has focused on cultural aspects of child development and education, including an international study of children's perspectives on their working lives.

Index